Bob the Builder
© HIT Entertainment PLC and Keith Chapman 2003.

A. B. C.

∞ FOR KIDS ∞

BUMPER SONGBOOK

100 SONGS

© Australian Broadcasting Corporation 2003

Bear In The Big Blue House created by Mitchell Kriegman - © 2003 The Jim Henson Company, JIM HENSON'S mark and logo, BEAR IN THE BIG BLUE HOUSE mark and logo, characters and elements are trademarks of The Jim Henson Company.
All rights reserved.

The Wiggles - © 2003 The Wiggles Touring Pty Ltd

Play School © Australian Broadcasting Corporation 2003

Exclusive Distributors for Australia & New Zealand to the Music Trade:
Music Sales Pty Limited
120 Rothschild Avenue,
Rosebery NSW 2018 Australia

Exclusive Distributors for Australia & New Zealand to the Book Trade:
Macmillan Distribution Services
53 Parkwest Drive
Derrimut VIC 3030 Australia

This book © Copyright 2003 Wise Publications
ISBN 1 876871 38 5
Order No MS04035
Printed By McPherson's Printing Group
Cover Design By Glen Hannah
Music Arrangements by Tony Celiberti (Scarlet Music)
With special thanks to Rachael Hammond at the ABC &
Sally Devenish at Pancake Press

Published in Australia under licence from the Australian Broadcasting Corporation
© Australian Broadcasting Corporation 2003.

Music Sales Pty Limited
Lisgar House Level 4, 32 Carrington St
Sydney NSW 2000 Australia

WISE PUBLICATIONS
London/NewYork/Sydney/Paris/Copenhagen/Madrid/Berlin

Bananas in Pyjamas © Australian Broadcasting Corporation 2003.
Original Song by Carey Blyton

CONTENTS

A Sailor Went To Diz

Traditional

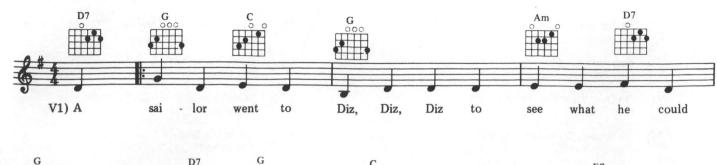

V1) A sai - lor went to Diz, Diz, Diz to see what he could

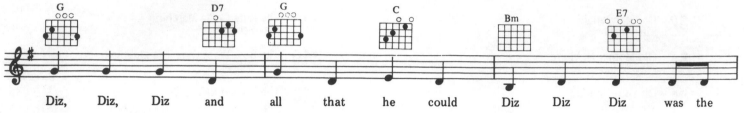

Diz, Diz, Diz and all that he could Diz Diz Diz was the

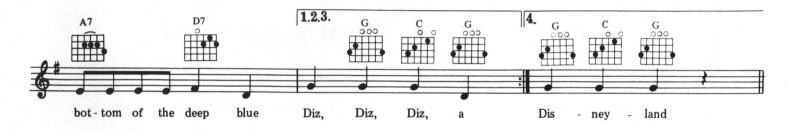

bot - tom of the deep blue Diz, Diz, Diz, a Dis - ney - land

V2. A sailor went to knee knee knee,
To see what he could knee knee knee,
And all that he could knee knee knee,
Was the bottom of the deep blue knee knee knee.

V3. A sailor went to land land land,
To see what he could land land land,
And all that he could land land land,
Was the bottom of the deep blue land land land

V4. A sailor went to Disneyland,
To see what he could Disneyland,
And all that he could Disneyland,
Was the bottom of the deep blue Disneyland!

Baa Baa Black Sheep
Traditional

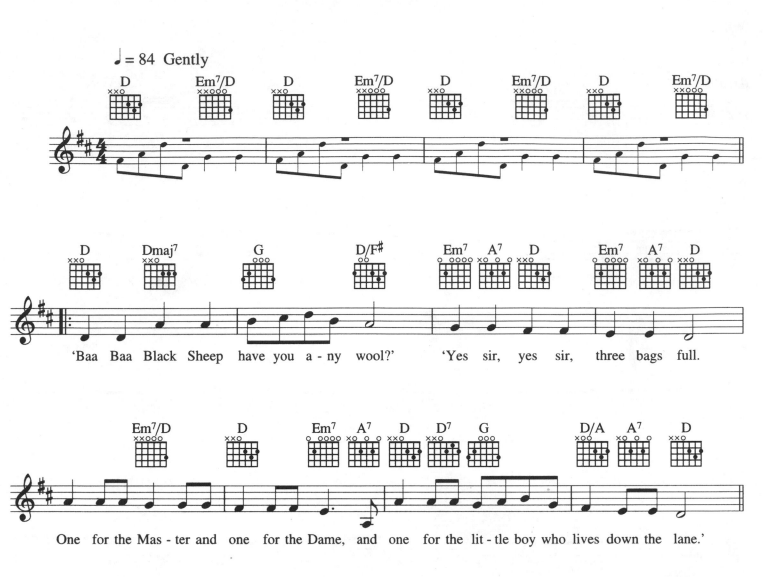

'Baa Baa Black Sheep have you a-ny wool?' 'Yes sir, yes sir, three bags full.

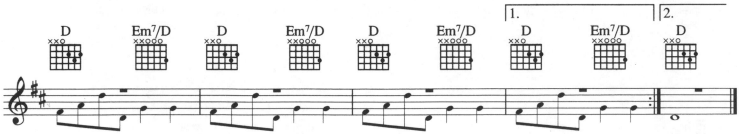

One for the Mas-ter and one for the Dame, and one for the lit-tle boy who lives down the lane.'

Bananas In Pyjamas

Carey Blyton

With a swing feel. ♪ ♪ = ♪. ♪

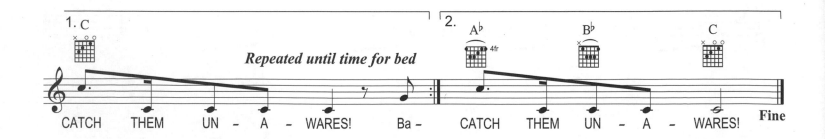

Bear Hunt

Traditional

Run through the gate! Shut the gate! In the door! Shut the door!

Whew! (We're never going on a bear hunt again!) uh – huh! **Fine**

(Additional lyrics)
* = repeat phrase

Verse 2

A forest!   *
A tall dark forest,   *
We can't go over it,   *
We can't go under it,   *
We'll have to go through it.   *
Stumble stumble trip! Stumble stumble trip!

Verse 3

Mud!   *
Thick oozy mud!   *
We can't go over it,   *
We can't go under it,   *
We'll have to go through it.   *
Squelsh, squelsh, squelsh, squelsh, squelsh,squelsh, squelsh!

Verse 4

A cave!   *
A dark, gloomy cave!   *
We can't go over it,   *
We can't go under it,   *
We'll have to go through it.   *
Tip toe, tip toe, tip toe, tip toe!

Bobby Bingo

Traditional

1. There
was a far-mer had a dog, his name was Bob-by Bin - go.

B - I - N - G - O, B - I - N - G - O,

B - I - N - G - O, his name was Bob - by Bin - go.

1.-3.

4.

2. 3. 4. There Bin - go.

Bumping and a-Jumping

Chris Harriott / Simon Hopkinson

11

Bunyip Groove

David Moye

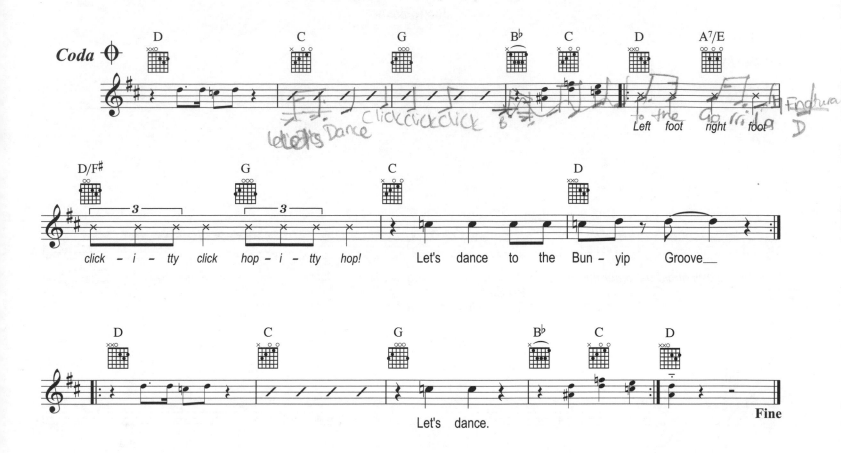

(Additional lyrics

Verse 2

Well come on everybody, lets wobble our knees.
We'll ride a big wave down by the sea.
We'll twist to the song by a billabong.
We'll do some movin and groovin jump and jive!

"C" Is For Cookie

Joe Raposo

Original key Eb Major

♩ = 120

Moderato

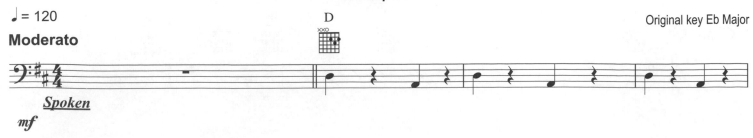

Spoken

mf

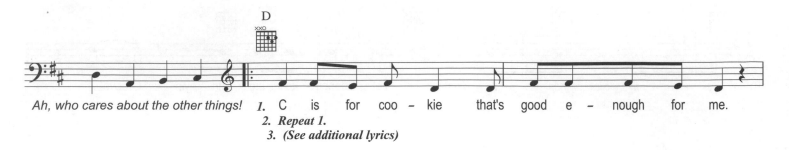

Ah, who cares about the other things!

1. C is for coo - kie that's good e - nough for me.
2. Repeat 1.
3. *(See additional lyrics)*

C is for cook - ie that's good e - nough for me.

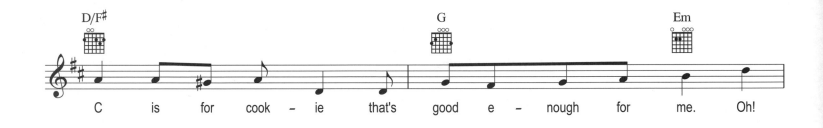

C is for cook - ie that's good e - nough for me. Oh!

1.2. / 3.

Coo - kie, cook - ie, cook - ie, starts with C. *Oh!*

C is for cook - ie, that's good e - nough for me. *Yeah!*

C is for cook-ie that's good e-nough for me. C is for cook-ie that's

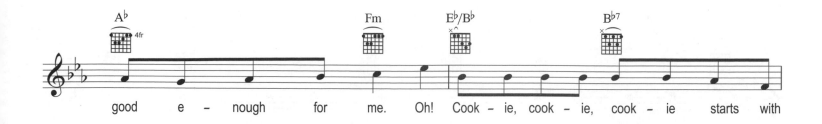

good e-nough for me. Oh! Cook-ie, cook-ie, cook-ie starts with

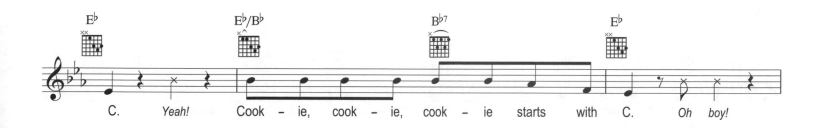

C. *Yeah!* Cook-ie, cook-ie, cook-ie starts with C. *Oh boy!*

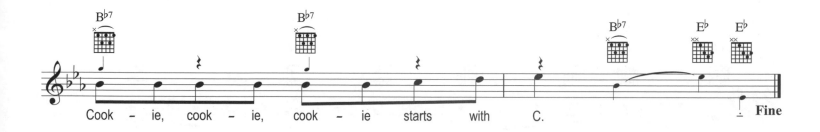

Cook-ie, cook-ie, cook-ie starts with C. **Fine**

(Additional lyrics)

Spoken

You know what?

A round doughnut with one bite out of it, also looks like a C
But it is not as good as a cookie!
Oh and the moon sometimes looks like a C, but you can't eat that!
So ...

Can We Fix It

Paul Joyce

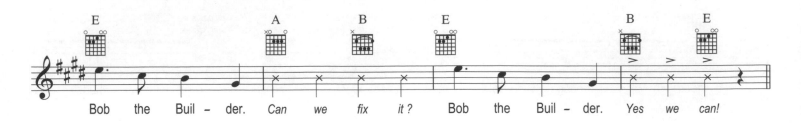

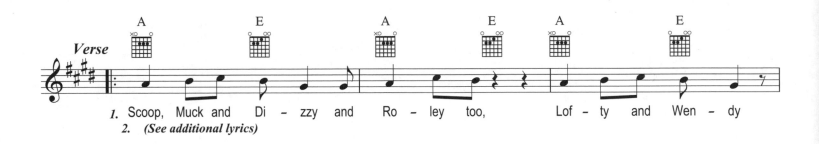

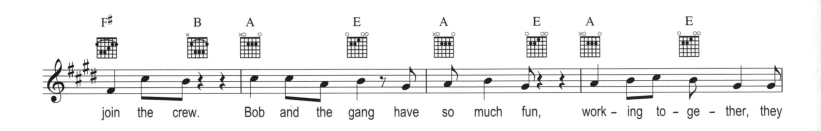

Can You (Point Your Fingers And Do The Twist?)

Murray Cook/Jeff Fatt/Anthony Field/Greg Page

(Additional lyrics)

Verse 2

Can you stand, on one foot and shake your hands?
Can you stand, on one foot and shake your hands?
Well we're gonna go up, then go down,
Get back up and turn around.
Can you stand, on one foot and shake your hands?

Verse 3
Repeat Verse 1.

Did You Ever See A Lassie

Traditional

1. Did you e - ver see a las - sie go this way and
2. Oh, you can't put your muck in our dust - bin, in

that way, did you e - ver see a - las - sie go
our dust - bin you can't put your muck in our dust - bin 'cause

this way and that? Go this way and that way and
our dust - bin's full! There's round ones and that square ones and

that way and this way, Did you e - ver see a
square ones and and this round ones, but you can't put your muck in

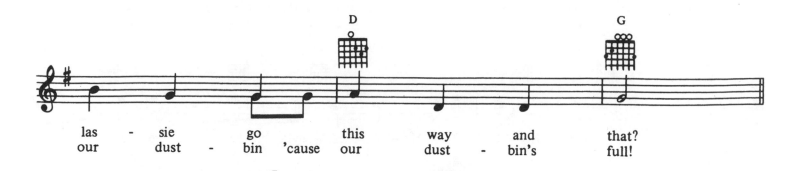

las - sie go this way and that?
our dust - bin 'cause our dust - bin's full!

D.O.R.O.T.H.Y. (My Favourite Dinosaur)

Murray Cook/Jeff Fatt/Anthony Field/Greg Page/John Field

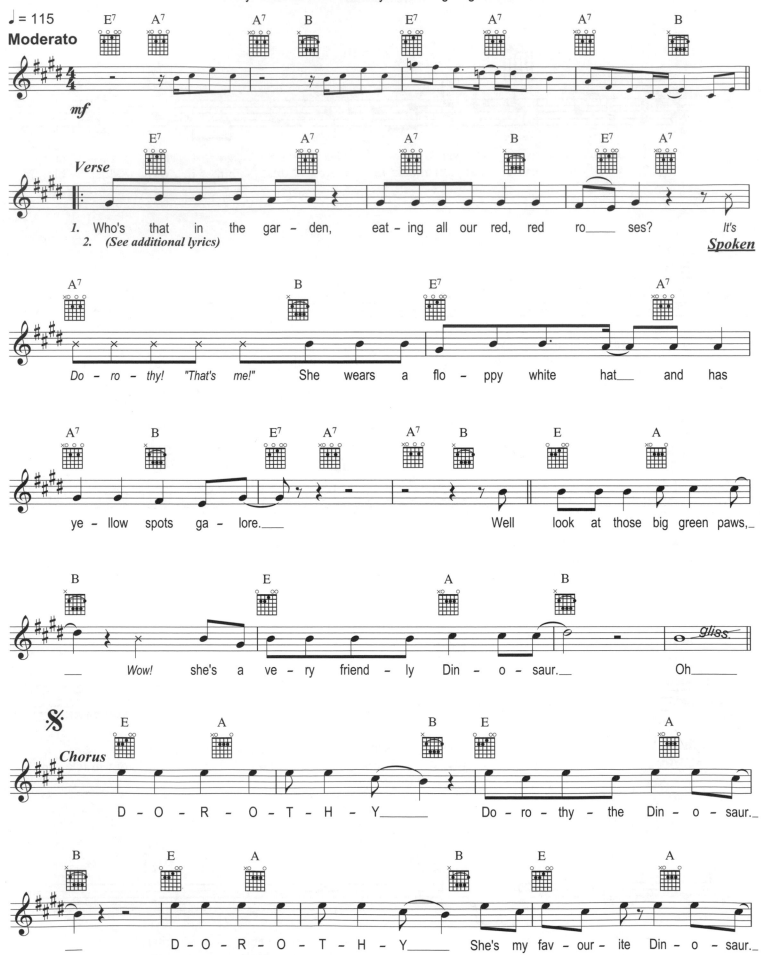

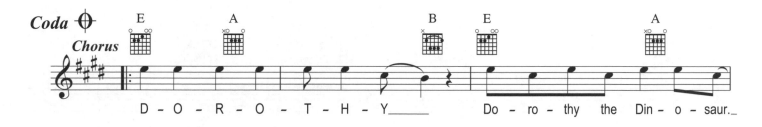

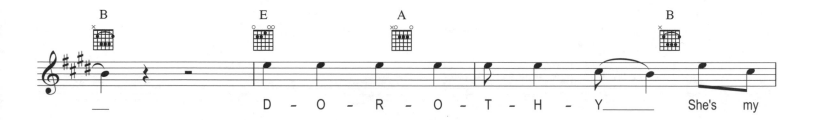

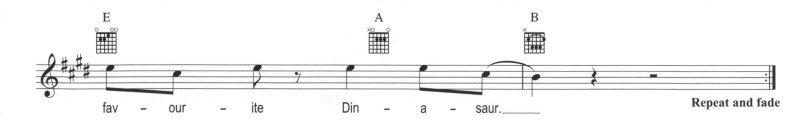

Repeat and fade

(Additional lyrics)

Verse 2

She's a really helpful Dinosaur, she works so hard in the garden.
She pulls out all the weeds, plants more roses and she mows the lawn.
When the music starts she dances on the floor,
She's a really groovy Dinosaur.

Doctor Knickerbocker

Traditional

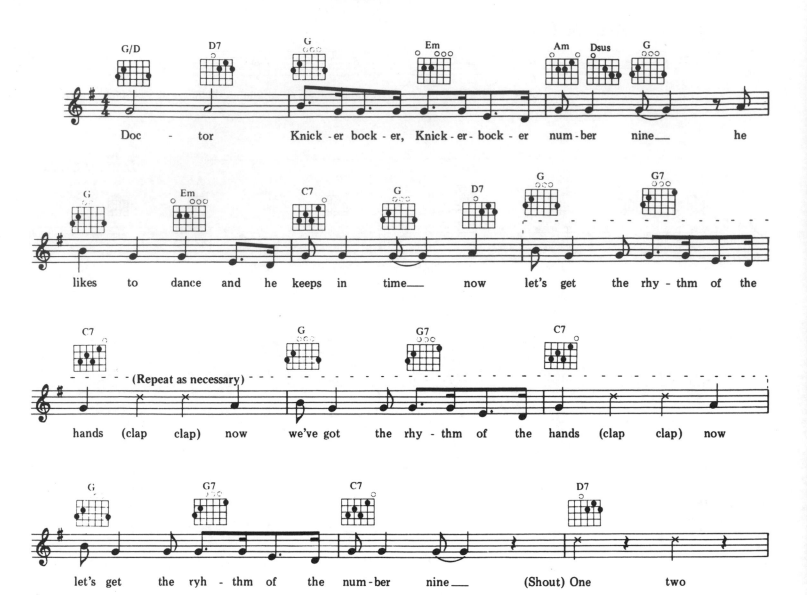

Doc - tor Knick - er bock - er, Knick - er - bock - er num - ber nine___ he

likes to dance and he keeps in time___ now let's get the rhy - thm of the

(Repeat as necessary)

hands (clap clap) now we've got the rhy - thm of the hands (clap clap) now

let's get the ryh - thm of the num - ber nine___ (Shout) One two

three four five six sev - en eight nine!

V2. Doctor Knickerbocker, Knickerbocker, number nine,
He likes to dance and he keeps in time,
Now lets get the rhythm of the feet (stamp stamp)
Now we've got the rhythm of the feet (stamp stamp)
Now lets get the rhythm of the hands (clap clap)
Now we've got the rhythm of the hands (clap clap)
Now lets get the rhythm of the number nine.
One, two, three four five six seven eight nine!

V3. Doctor Knickerbocker, Knickerbocker, number nine,
He likes to dance and he keeps in time,
Now lets get the rhythm of the hips (wolf whistle)
Now we've got the rhythm of the hips (wolf whistle)
Now lets get the rhythm of the feet (stamp stamp)
Now we've got the rhythm of the feet (stamp stamp)
Now lets get the rhythm of the hands (clap clap)
Now we've got the rhythm of the hands (clap clap)
Now lets get the rhythm of the number nine.
One, two, three four five six seven eight nine!

V4. Doctor Knickerbocker, Knickerbocker, number nine,
He likes to dance and he keeps in time,
Now lets get the rhythm of the lips (Kiss kiss)
Now we've got the rhythm of the lips (kiss kiss) . . . . . etc.

V5. Doctor Knickerbocker, Knickerbocker, number nine,
He likes to dance and he keeps in time,
Now lets get the rhythm of the head (nod nod)
Now we've got the rhythm of the head (nod nod) . . . . etc.

Five Green Bottles

Traditional

With a swing feel.

Original key Bb Major

Moderato ♩ = 122

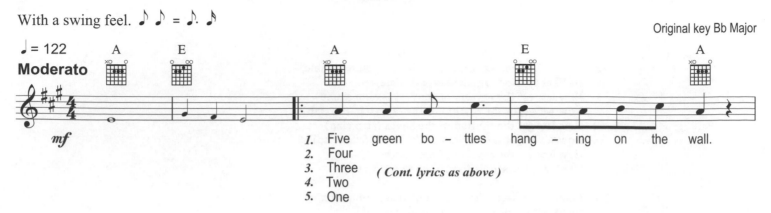

mf

1. Five green bo-ttles hang-ing on the wall.
2. Four
3. Three *(Cont. lyrics as above)*
4. Two
5. One

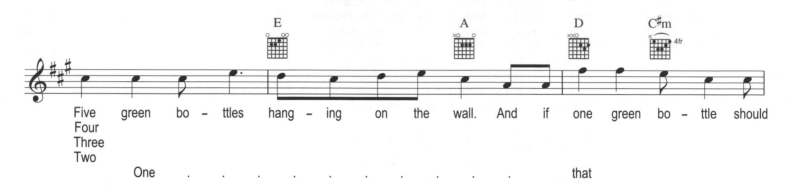

Five green bo-ttles hang-ing on the wall. And if one green bo-ttle should
Four
Three
Two
One . . . . that

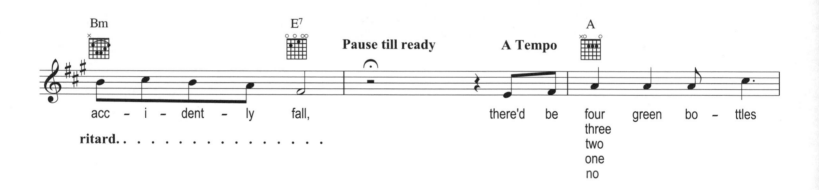

Pause till ready   A Tempo

acc-i-dent-ly fall,   there'd be four green bo-ttles
ritard. . . . . three
two
one
no

1. 2. 3. 4.   5.

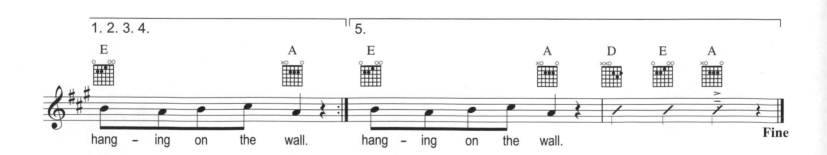

hang-ing on the wall.   hang-ing on the wall.

Fine

24

Five Little Ducks

Traditional

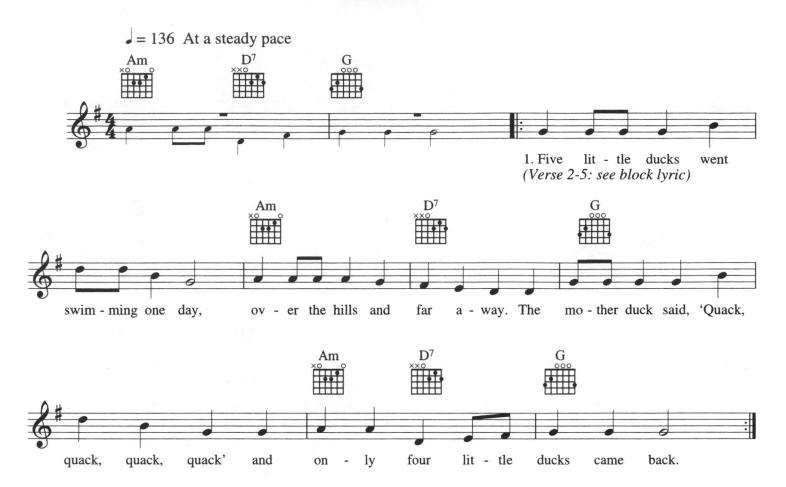

♩ = 136 At a steady pace

1. Five lit - tle ducks went
(Verse 2-5: see block lyric)

swim - ming one day, ov - er the hills and far a - way. The mo - ther duck said, 'Quack,

quack, quack, quack' and on - ly four lit - tle ducks came back.

Verse 2:

Four little ducks went swimming one day,
Over the hills and far away.
The mother duck said, 'Quack, quack, quack, quack.'
And only three little ducks came back.

Verse 3:

Three little ducks went swimming one day,
Over the hills and far away.
The mother duck said, 'Quack, quack, quack, quack.'
And only two little ducks came back.

Verse 4:

Two little ducks went swimming one day,
Over the hills and far away.
The mother duck said, 'Quack, quack, quack, quack.'
And only one little duck came back.

Verse 5:

One little duck went swimming one day,
Over the hills and far away.
The mother duck said, 'Quack, quack, quack, quack.'
And five little ducks came swimming right back.

Flower Pot Time

P. Barton/The Flowerpot Gang

Original key Bb Major

(Additional lyrics)

Verse 2

Well there's lots of flowers and lots of sun,
And everybody's having so much fun.
Phil's bopping and Dan's rocking and Christie sings and dances all day.

Frère Jacques

Traditional

Georgie Porgie

Traditional

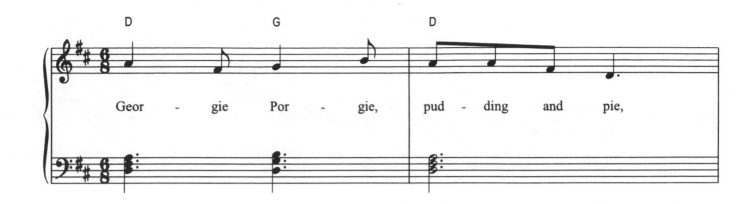

Geor - gie Por - gie, pud - ding and pie,

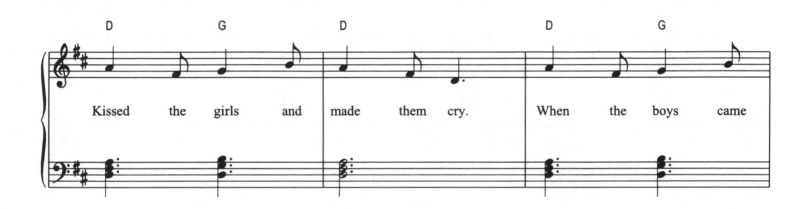

Kissed the girls and made them cry. When the boys came

out to play, Geor - gie Por - gie ran a - way.

Fruit Salad

Murray Cook/Jeff Fatt/Anthony Field/Greg Page

Fruit sa - lad, yumm - y, yumm - y!

Yumm - y, yumm - y, yumm - y, yumm - y fruit sa - lad!_____ Let's make some fruit

sa - lad to - day, (ah ha ha) it's fun to do it's the health - y way. (ah ha ha)

(Background vocals)

Take all the fruit that you want to eat, it's going to be a fruit

sa - lad treat!_____ (The first *1.* step) Peel your ba - na - nas. (The se - cond

2. (See additional lyrics)

step) Toss in some grapes.__ (The third__ step) Chop up some app - les.

Chop up some mel - ons and put them on your plate.____ Now we've made it, it's

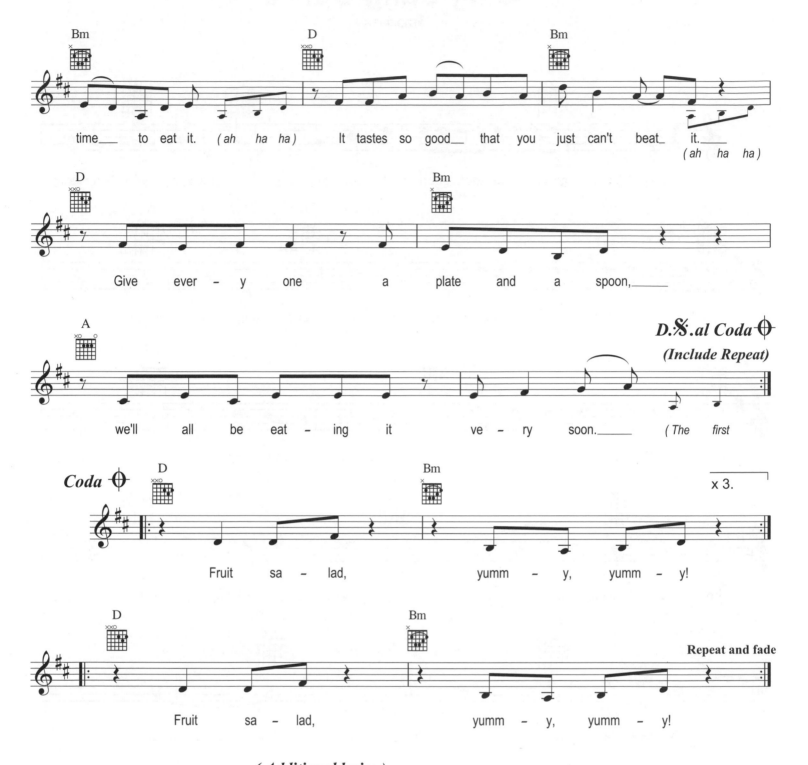

(Additional lyrics)

2. *(The first step)*   Eat up the banana.
    (The second step)   Eat up some grapes.
    (The third step)   Eat up some apples.
    Eat up the melons now there's nothing on your plate.

    Now we've had our fruit salad today, *(ah ha ha)*
    It's time to put the scraps away. *(ah ha ha)*
    Wash the bowls and wash the spoons,
    Let's do it all again real soon.

Ging Gang Goolie

Traditional

Ging - gang goo-li gooli gooli gooli wash wash ging gang goo, ging gang goo. Ging gang

gooli gooli gooli gooli wash wash ging gang goo, ging gang goooo!

Hey - la, _____ oh hey la shey la _____ oh hey-la shey - la

ho la ho _____ hey - la _____ oh hey-la shey-la _____

_____ oh hey la shey - la ho - la ho. _____

Shal - la wal - ly shal - la wal - ly shal - la wal - ly shal - la wal - ly

oom - pah oom - pah oom - pah oom - pah oom - pah oom - pah pah

Grand Old Duke Of York

Traditional

♩ = 100 Military march

Oh, the Grand Old Duke of York, he had ten thou-sand men. He marched them up to the top of the hill and he marched them down a-gain. And when they were up they were up, and when they were down they were down, And when they were on-ly half-way up they were nei-ther up nor down.

Oh, the

Have You Seen The Muffin Man?

Traditional

Have you seen the Muf-fin Man, the Muf-fin Man, the Muf-fin Man? Oh,

(Verse 2: see block lyric)

have you seen the Muf-fin Man who lives down Dru-ry Lane?

Oh,

3. Have you seen the Muf-fin Man, the Muf-fin Man, the Muf-fin Man? Oh,

have you seen the Muf-fin Man who lives down Dru-ry Lane? Oh

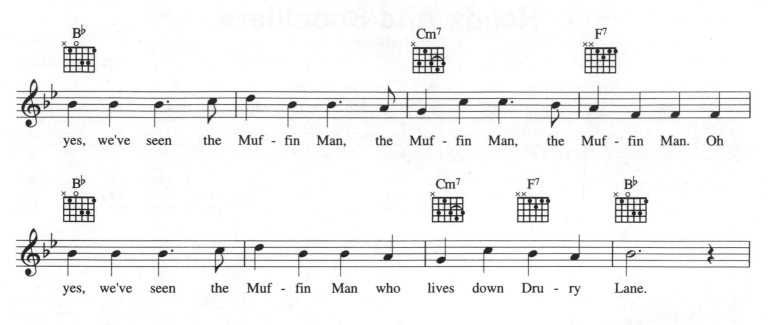

yes, we've seen the Muf - fin Man, the Muf - fin Man, the Muf - fin Man. Oh

yes, we've seen the Muf - fin Man who lives down Dru - ry Lane.

Verse 2:

Oh yes, I've seen the Muffin Man,
The Muffin Man, The Muffin Man.
Oh yes, I've seen the Muffin Man
Who lives down Drury Lane.

Heads And Shoulders

Traditional

Original key Bb Major

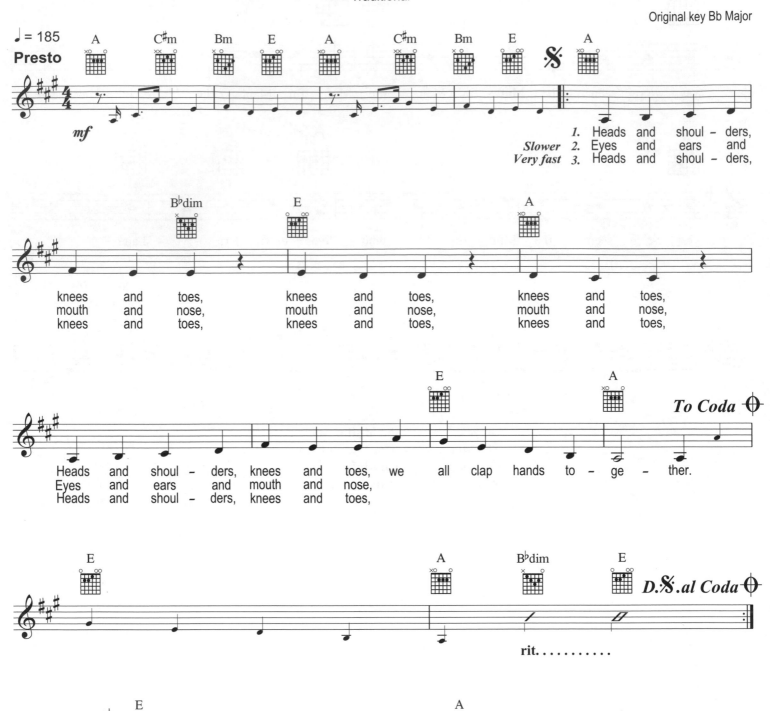

Here Comes A Bear

Murray Cook/Jeff Fatt/Anthony Field/Greg Page

With a swing feel. ♪ ♪ = ♪. ♪

♩ = 130

Moderato

Verse

1. Here comes a bear, stomp - ing, stomp - ing. A ve - ry sca - rey bear,

2. 3. 4. 5. (See additional lyrics)

stomp - ing, stomp - ing. Paws up in the air, stomp - ing, stomp - ing.

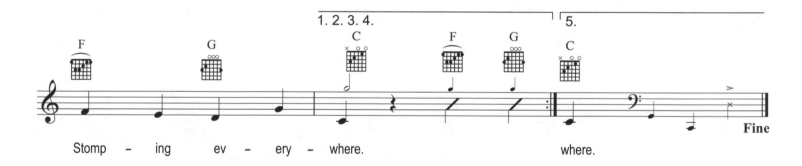

Stomp - ing ev - ery - where. where.

Fine

(Additional lyrics)

Verse 2
Kangaroo jumps, boing, boing!   He jumps so high, boing, boing!
He almost touched the sky, boing, boing!   The kangaroo jumps so high.

Verse 3
Here comes a snake, Sss, Sss!   Slithering along, Sss, Sss!
His body's very long, Sss, Sss!   Slippery snake slithers along.

Verse 4
Wombat crawls, crawling, crawling!   Nose to the ground, crawling, crawling!
He's making lots of sound, crawling, crawling!   Crawling everywhere.

Verse 5
Repeat verse 1.

Hello

The Hooley Dooleys

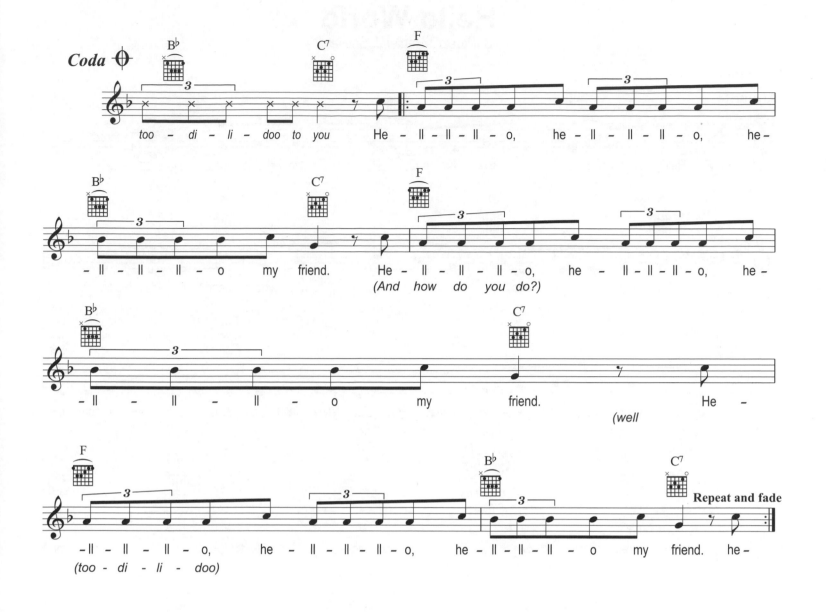

(Additional lyrics)

Verse 2

I'm Tickle the dudette.
Whenever I meet, somebody I know,
I always shake their hands and say hello!

Verse 3

We're the Hooley Dooleys, and how do you do?
We live near Tickle, and Russell the Kangaroo.
Whenever we meet, somebody we know,
We always shake their hands and say hello!

Hello World

B. Perez/P. Renier/J. Soulier

Henry The Octopus

Murray Cook/Jeff Fatt/Anthony Field/Greg Page

had no end. He will bake roast and fry, his fav – our – ite dish is

Chorus

sea – weed pie. Hen – ry the Oc – to – pus, lives down in the

dep blue sea Hen – ry the Oc – to – pus, he's a friend to

1. you and me   2. you and me

Fine

(Additional lyrics)

Verse 3
Henry has a happy smile
He'd like you to stay for a while
He'll put on his shoes and his eight legged pants
And show you all the tentacle dance

Here We Go Round The Mulberry Bush

Traditional

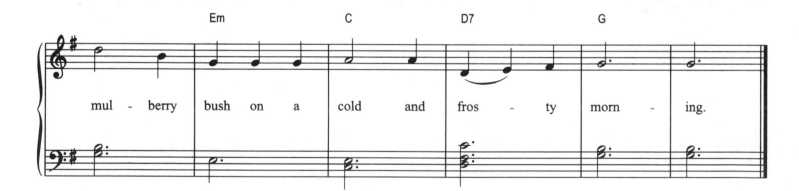

2. This is the way we wash our hands…
3. This is the way we wash our clothes…
4. This is the way we dry our clothes…
5. This is the way we iron our clothes…
6. This is the way we sweep the floor…
7. This is the way we brush our hair…
8. This is the way we go to school…
9. This is the way we come back from school…

Humpty Dumpty

Traditional

♩. = 86 Brightly

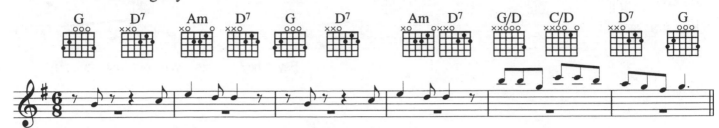

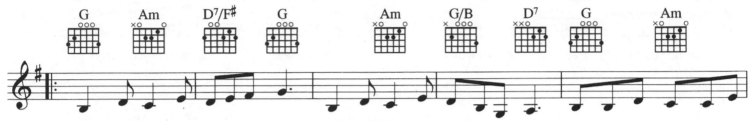

1. Hump-ty Dump-ty sat on a wall, Hump-ty Dump-ty had a great fall. All the King's hor-ses and
2. Hump-ty Dump-ty sat on the ground, Hump-ty Dump-ty looked all a-round. Gone were the chim-neys and

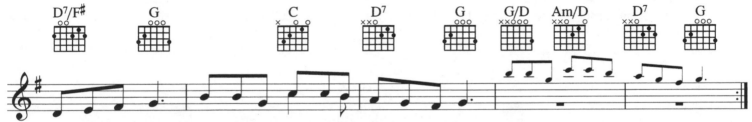

all the King's men, Could-n't put Hump-ty to - ge - ther a-gain.
gone were the roofs, All he could see were buck-les and hooves.

3. Hump-ty Dump-ty coun-ted to ten, Hump-ty Dump-ty got up a - gain.

molto rall.

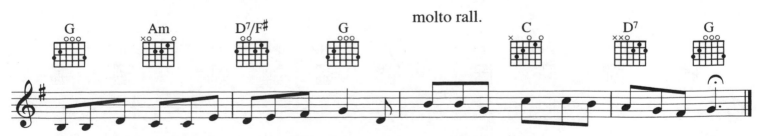

All the King's hor-ses and all the King's men Were hap-py that Hump-ty's to-ge-ther a-gain.

Hey Hey Are You Ready To Play (Tweenies Theme)

Pike/Kitchen/Brenton/Lauchlan

With a swing feel.

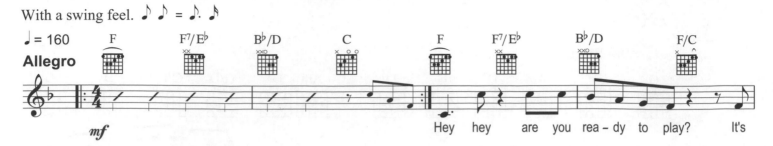

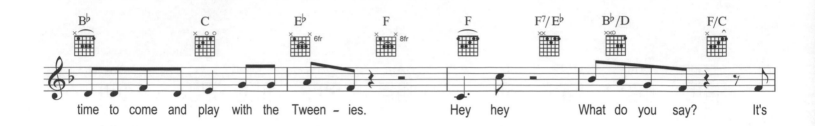

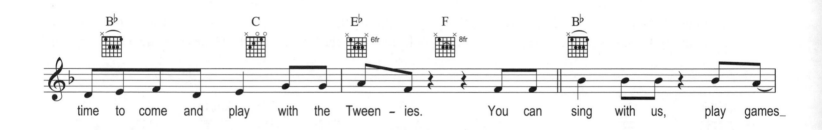

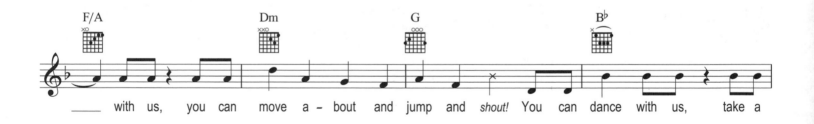

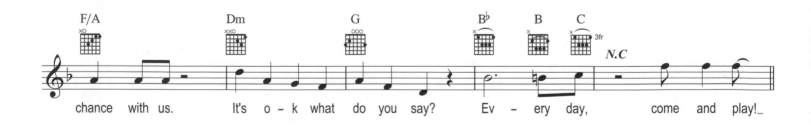

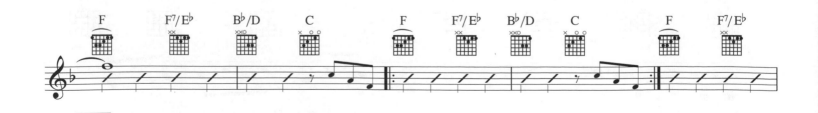

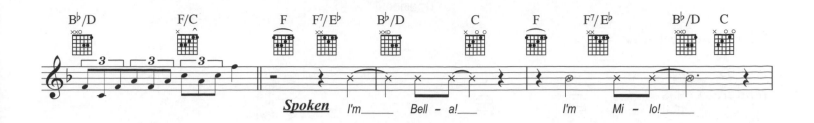

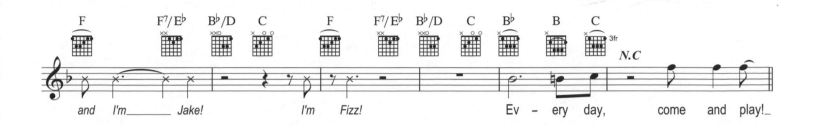

Spoken I'm_____ Bell - a!___ I'm Mi - lo!_____

and I'm_____ Jake! I'm Fizz! Ev - ery day, come and play!_

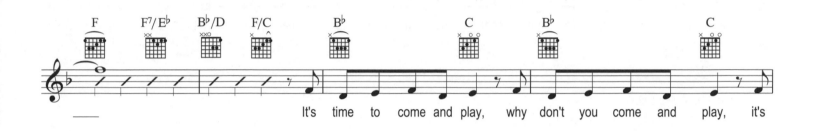

_____ It's time to come and play, why don't you come and play, it's

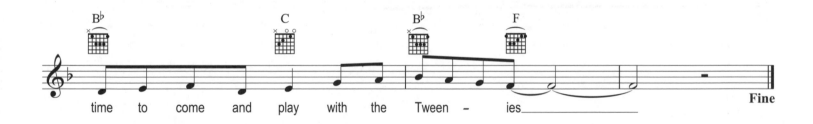

time to come and play with the Tween - ies_____ **Fine**

Hokey Pokey

Traditional

With a swing feel. ♪ ♪ = ♪. ♪

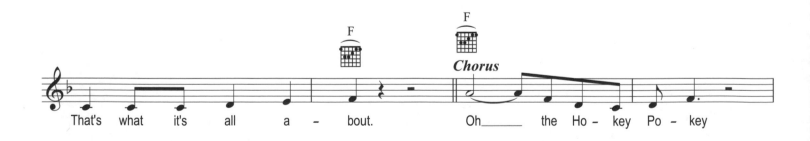

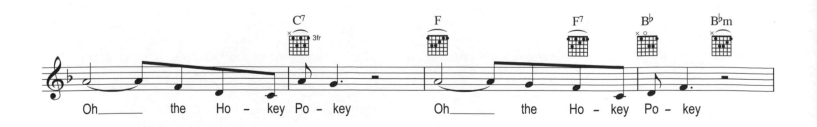

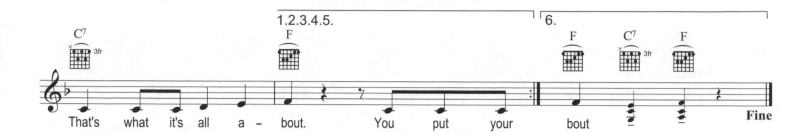

(Additional lyrics)

Verse 2

You put your left arm in, you put your left arm out, you put your left arm in and you shake it all about.
You do the Hokey Pokey and you turn around, that's what it's all about.

Verse 3

You put your right foot in, you put your right foot out, you put your right foot in and you shake it all about
 You do the Hokey Pokey and you turn around, that's what it's all about.

Verse 4

You put your left foot in, you put your left foot out, you put your left foot in and you shake it all about
You do the Hokey Pokey and you turn around, that's what it's all about.

Verse 5

You put your head in, you put your head out, you put your head in and you shake it all about
 You do the Hokey Pokey and you turn around, that's what it's all about.

Verse 6

You put your whole self in, you put your whole self out, you put your whole self in and you shake it all about
You do the Hokey Pokey and you turn around, that's what it's all about.

Home Among The Gumtrees

W. Johnson/B. Brown

2. I'll be standing in the kitchen
   Cooking up a roast,
   With Vegemite on toast,
   Just me and you, a cockatoo,
   And after tea we'll settle down
   Beside the hitching post,
   And watch the wombats play.

3. Some people like their houses built
   With fences all around,
   Others live in mansions,
   Or in bunkers underground,
   But I won't be content
   Until the day that I have found
   The place I long to be.

Hooray For Mr Whiskers

Franciscus Henry

With a swing feel. ♪ ♪ = ♪. ♪
♩ = 130

Moderato

mf When
1. Mis – ter Whis – kers comes to town, Hoo – ray for Mis – ter Whis – kers!
2. Mis – ter Whis – kers has three hats, Hoo – ray for Mis – ter Whis – kers!

Child – ren sing and dance a – round, Hoo – ray for Mis – ter Whis – kers! The
Some are round and some are fat, Hoo – ray for Mis – ter Whis – kers! A –

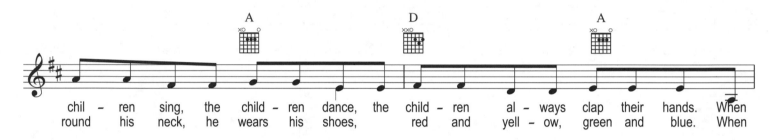

chil – ren sing, the child – ren dance, the child – ren al – ways clap their hands. When
round his neck, he wears his shoes, red and yell – ow, green and blue. When

Mis – ter Whis – kers comes to town, Hoo – ray for Mis – ter Whis – kers!

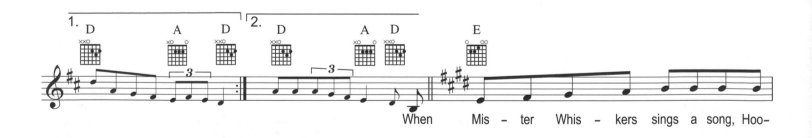

1. D A D   2. D A D   E

When Mis – ter Whis – kers sings a song, Hoo-

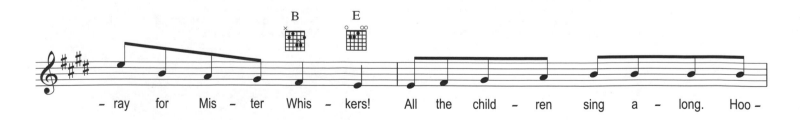

B E

– ray for Mis – ter Whis – kers! All the child – ren sing a – long. Hoo-

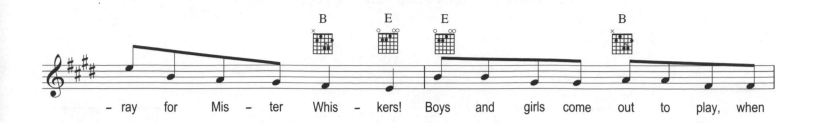

-ray for Mis – ter Whis – kers! Boys and girls come out to play, when

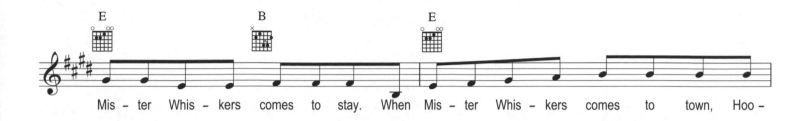

Mis – ter Whis – kers comes to stay. When Mis – ter Whis – kers comes to town, Hoo –

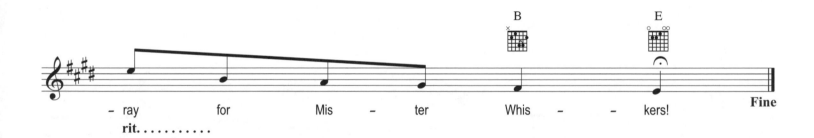

-ray for Mis – ter Whis – kers! Hoo – ray for Mis – ter Whis – kers! Hoo–

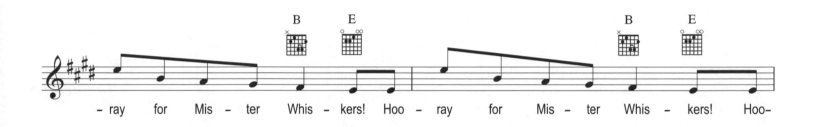

-ray for Mis – ter Whis – – kers! **Fine**

rit. . . . .

Hot Potato

Murray Cook/Jeff Fatt/Anthony Field/Greg Page/John Field

With a swing feel. ♪ ♪ = ♪. ♪

♩ = 180

Moderato

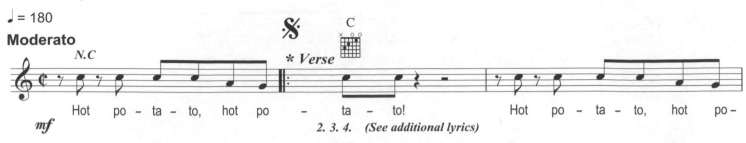

Hot po – ta – to, hot po – ta – to! Hot po – ta – to, hot po –

2. 3. 4. (See additional lyrics)

– ta – to! Hot po – ta – to, hot po – ta – to, po –

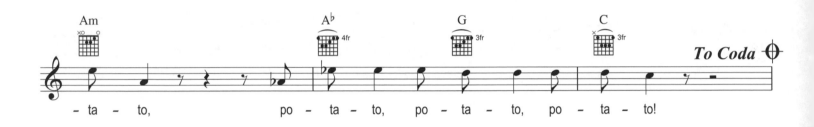

To Coda

– ta – to, po – ta – to, po – ta – to, po – ta – to!

Cold spag – he – tti, cold spag – Ooh wig – gy, wig – gy, wig – gy,

Ooh wig – gy, wig – gy, wig – gy, Give me that give me that, give me that food.

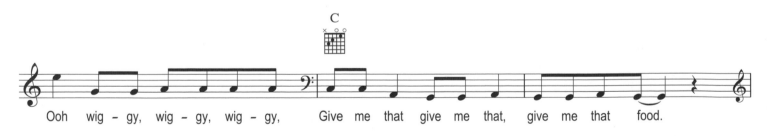

Ooh wig – gy, wig – gy, wig – gy Ooh wig – gy, wig – gy, wig – gy,

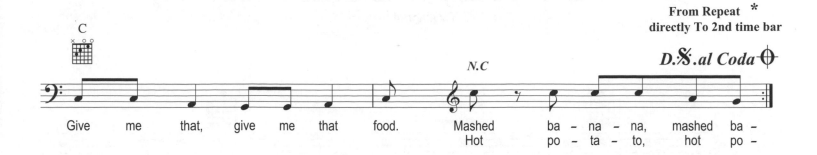

Give me that, give me that food. Mashed ba – na – na, mashed ba –
Hot po – ta – to, hot po –

Fine

(Additional lyrics)

* = repeat phrase

Verse 2

Cold spaghetti, cold spaghetti!   *
Cold spaghetti, cold spaghetti!   *
Cold spaghetti, cold
Spaghetti!   *
Spaghetti!   *
Spaghetti, spaghetti, spaghetti!

Verse 3.

Mashed banana, mashed banana!   *
Mashed banana, mashed banana!   *
Mashed banana, mashed
Banana!   *
Banana!   *
Banana, banana, banana!

Verse 4.
repeat verse 1.

I Know An Old Lady Who Swallowed A Fly

Traditional

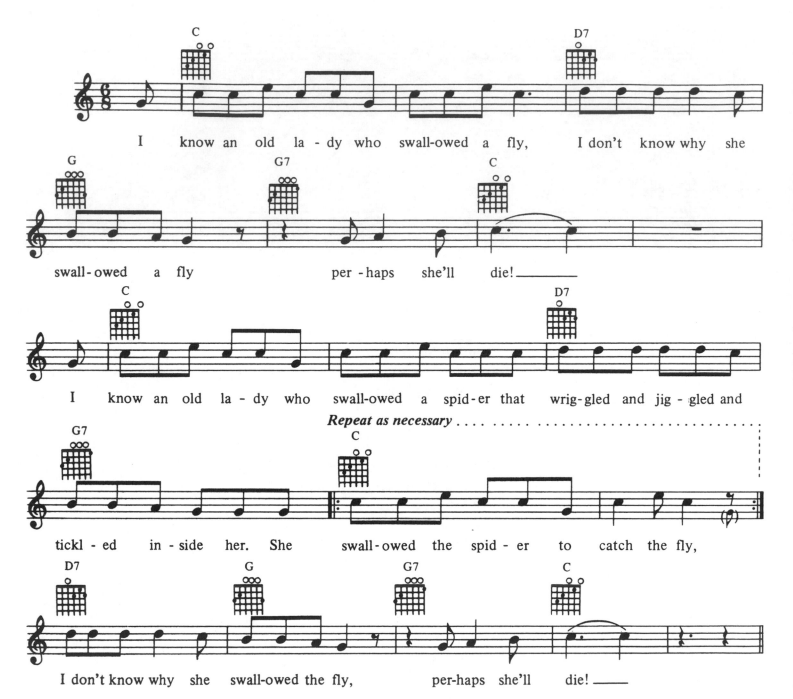

I know an old la - dy who swall-owed a fly, I don't know why she swall-owed a fly per - haps she'll die!

I know an old la - dy who swall-owed a spid-er that wrig-gled and jig - gled and

Repeat as necessary . . . .

tickl - ed in - side her. She swall-owed the spid - er to catch the fly,

I don't know why she swall-owed the fly, per-haps she'll die!

3. I know an old lady who swallowed a bird.
How absurd, to swallow a bird!
She swallowed the bird to catch the spider
That wriggled. . . . etc.

4. I know an old lady who swallowed a cat,
Just fancy that, she swallowed a cat!
She swallowed the cat to catch the bird,
She swallowed the bird to catch the spider
That wriggled. . . . etc.

5. I know an old lady who swallowed a dog,
What a hog, to swallow a dog!
She swallowed the dog to catch the cat,
She swallowed the cat. . . . etc.

6. I know an old lady who swallowed a goat.
She just opened her throat and swallowed a goat!
She swallowed the goat to catch the dog,
She swallowed the dog. . . . etc.

7. I know an old lady who swallowed a cow.
I don't know HOW she swallowed a cow.
She swallowed the cow to catch the goat,
She swallowed the goat. . . . etc.

8. I know an old lady who swallowed a rhinoceros,
THAT'S PREPOSTEROUS! !
She swallowed the rhino to catch the cow,
She swallowed the cow. . . . etc.

9. I know an old lady who swallowed a horse.
She's dead of course.

I'm A Little Teapot

Clarence Kelley & George H. Sanders

I'm a lit - tle tea - pot, short and stout. Here's my han - dle,
(Verse 2 & 3: see block lyric)

here's my___ spout. When I get all steamed up hear me shout,

Tip me ov - er, pour me out! Tip me ov - er,

pour me out! pour me out!

Verse 2:

I'm a tube of toothpaste on the shelf,
I get so lonely all by myself.
When it gets to night time then I shout,
Just lift my lid off, squeeze me out!
Lift my lid off, squeeze me out!

Verse 3:

I'm a little teapot, short and stout.
Here's my handle, here's my spout.
When I get all steamed up, hear me shout,
Tip me over, pour me out!
Tip me over, pour me out!

If You're Happy And You Know It

Traditional

4. If you're happy and you know it,
   shout hurray - HURRAY
   If you're happy and you know it,
   shout hurray - HURRAY
   If you're happy and you know it,
   you really ought to show it
   If you're happy and you know it,
   shout hurray, stamp your feet,
   nod your head, clap your hands.

5. If you're happy and you know it,
   clap your hands - CLAP CLAP
   If you're happy and you know it,
   clap your hands - CLAP CLAP
   If you're happy and you know it,
   you really ought to show it
   If you're happy and you know it,
   clap your hands, shout hurray,
   stamp your feet, nod your head,
   clap your hands.

Jack And Jill

Traditional

Incy Wincy Spider

Traditional

The een - sy ween - sy spi -

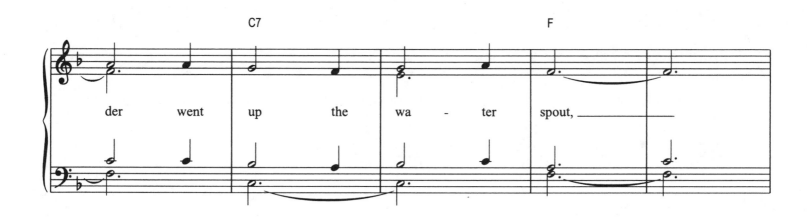

der went up the wa - ter spout, _____

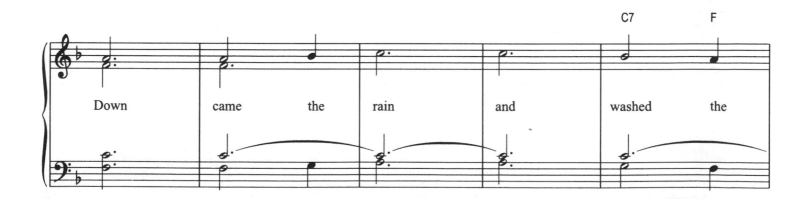

Down came the rain and washed the

Kookaburra Sits In The Old Gumtree

Marion Sinclair

1. Kook - a - burr - a sits in the old gum tree ___
2. Kook - a - burr - a sits in the old gum tree ___
3. Kook - a - burr - a sits on the elec - tric wire ___
4. Kook - a - burr - a sits at the M. C. G. ___

Mer - ry Mer - ry king of the bush is he ___ Laugh, Kook - a - burr - a,
Eat - ing all the gum drops ___ he can see ___ Stop, Kook - a - burr - a,
Tears ___ in his eyes and his pants on fire ___ Ouch! Kook - a - burr - a,
Watch-ing the crick - et on T. V. ___ Bored, Kook - a - burr - a,.

laugh, Kook - a - burr - a, Gay your life must be.
stop, Kook - a - burr - a, Leave some there for me.
Ouch! Kook - a - burr - a, Hot your tail must be.
Bored, Kook - a - burr - a, They've all stopped for tea.

Lavender's Blue

Traditional

Lav - en - der's blue, dil - ly, dil - ly, Lav - en - der's

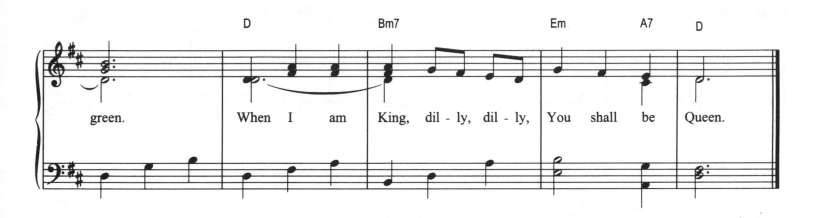

green. When I am King, dil - ly, dil - ly, You shall be Queen.

2.   Call up your men, dilly dilly,
Set them to work.
Some to the plough, dilly dilly,
Some to the cart.

3.   Some to make hay, dilly, dilly,
Some to cut corn.
Whilst you and I, dilly, dilly,
Keep ourselves warm.

4.   Roses are red, dilly, dilly,
Violets are blue.
If you love me, dilly, dilly,
I will love you.

5.   Let the birds sing, dilly, dilly,
And the lambs play.
We shall be safe, dilly, dilly,
Out of harm's way.

Little Bo-Peep

Traditional

Lit - tle Bo - Peep has lost her sheep and does - n't know where ____ to find them. Leave them a - lone and they'll ____ come home, bring - ing their tails ____ be - hind them.

2. Little Bo-Peep fell fast asleep
   And dreamed she heard them bleating.
   But when she awoke, she found it a joke,
   For they were still a-fleeting.

3. Then up she took, her little crook,
   Determined for to find them.
   She found them indeed, but it made her heart bleed,
   For they'd left their tails behind them.

Little Peter Rabbit

Traditional

Little Miss Muffet

Traditional

Gently ♩ = 66

Lit - tle Miss Muf - fet   sat on her tuf - fet,   eat - ing her curds and whey.   There

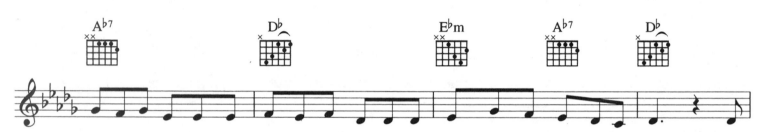

came a big spi - der which   sat down be - side her and   fright - ened Miss Muf - fet a - way.   And

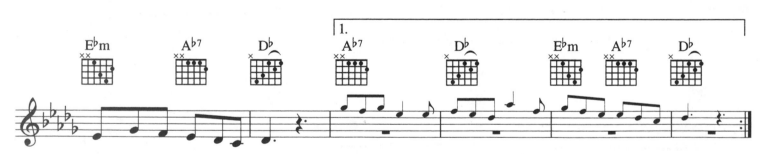

1.

fright - ened Miss Muf - fet a - way.

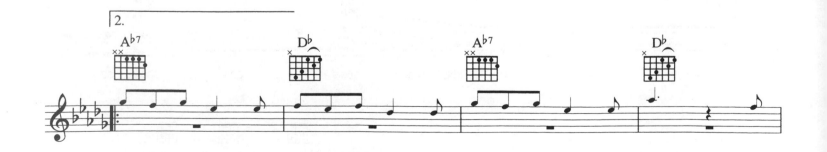

2.

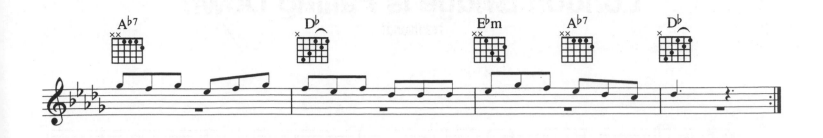

Lit - tle Miss Muf - fet sat on her tuf - fet, eat - ing her curds and whey. There

came a big spi - der which sat down be - side her and fright - ened Miss Muf - fet a -

rit.

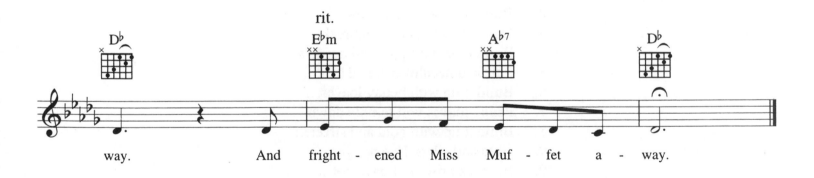

way.   And fright - ened Miss Muf - fet a - way.

London Bridge Is Falling Down

Traditional

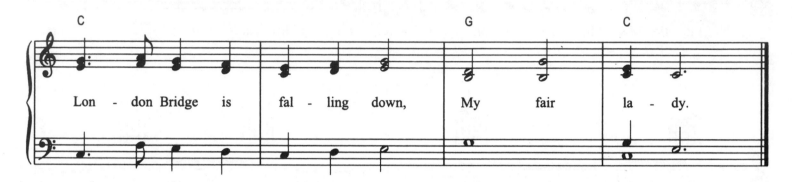

2. Build it up with iron bars…
3. Iron bars will bend and break…
4. Build it up with pins and needles…
5. Pins and needles rust and bend…
6. Build it up with penny loaves…
7. Penny loaves will tumble down…
8. Build it up with gold and silver…
9. Gold and silver I've not got…
10. Here's a prisoner I have got…
11. What's the prisoner done to you?…
12. Stole my watch and broke my chain…
13. What'll you take to set him free?…
14. One hundred pounds will set him free…
15. One hundred pounds we have not got…
16. Then off to prison he must go…

Looby Loo

Traditional

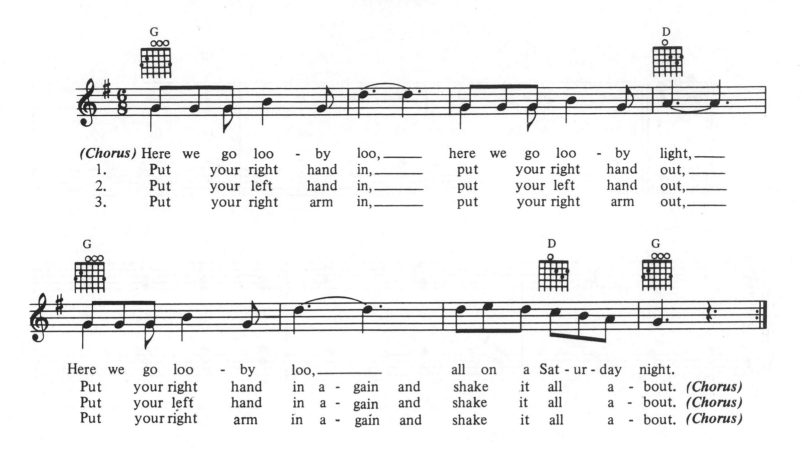

(Chorus) Here we go loo - by loo, _____ here we go loo - by light, _____
1. Put your right hand in, _____ put your right hand out, _____
2. Put your left hand in, _____ put your left hand out, _____
3. Put your right arm in, _____ put your right arm out, _____

Here we go loo - by loo, _____ all on a Sat - ur - day night.
Put your right hand in a - gain and shake it all a - bout. *(Chorus)*
Put your left hand in a - gain and shake it all a - bout. *(Chorus)*
Put your right arm in a - gain and shake it all a - bout. *(Chorus)*

4. Put your left arm in,
   Put your left arm out
   Put your left arm in again
   And shake it all about.
(Chorus)
5. Put your right foot in,
   Put your right foot out,
   Put your right foot in again
   And shake it all about.
(Chorus)
6. Put your left foot in. . . .
(Chorus)
7. Right leg
(Chorus)
8. Left leg
(Chorus)
9. Back
(Chorus)
10. Front
(Chorus)
11. Head
(Chorus)

Mary Had A Little Lamb

Traditional

2. And everywhere that Mary went,
    Mary went, Mary went,
    Everywhere that Mary went
    The lamb was sure to go.

3. It followed her to school one day,
    School one day, school one day,
    Followed her to school one day,
    That was against the rule.

4. It made the children laugh and play,
    Laugh and play, laugh and play,
    Made the children laugh and play
    To see the lamb at school.

Mr Squiggle (Main Theme)

J & G Ayling

With a swing feel. ♪ ♪ = ♪. ♪

♩ = 120

Moderato

mf

C

Here's Mis - ter Squi - ggle, with

G⁷

lots of fun for ev - ery one. Here's Mis - ter Squi - ggle,

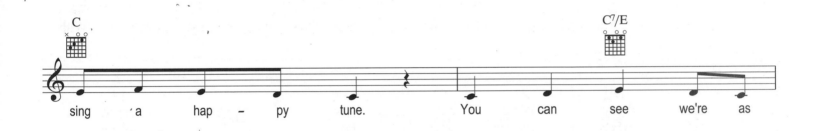

C   C⁷/E

sing a hap - py tune.   You can see we're as

F   F♯dim

hap - py as can be.   Mis - ter

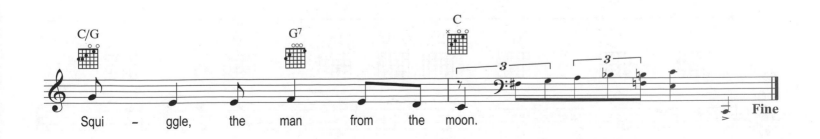

C/G   G⁷   C

Squi - ggle, the man from the moon.   Fine

Mary, Mary Quite Contrary

Traditional

Ma - ry, Ma - ry, quite con - tra - ry, how does your gar - den grow? "With

sil - ver bells and cock - le shells and pret - ty maids all in a row.

Michael Finnegan

Traditional

Lively Hillbilly ♩ = 110

1. There

was an old man called Mi - chael Fin - ne - gan, He grew whisk- ers on his chin - ne - gan. The
was an old man called Mi - chael Fin - ne - gan, He went fish - ing with a pin a - gain. He

wind came up and blew them in a - gain. Poor old Michael Fin - ne - gan. Be - gin a - gain.
caught a fish then dropped it in a - gain! Poor old Michael Fin - ne - gan. Be - gin a - gain.

1.

2. There

74

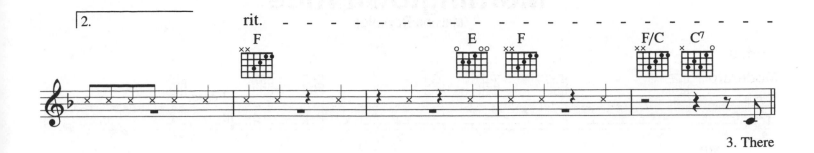

3. There

Sad and Slow ♩ = 92

was an old man called Mi - chael Fin - ne - gan, He grew fat then he grew thin a - gain.

Tempo Primo ♩ = 110

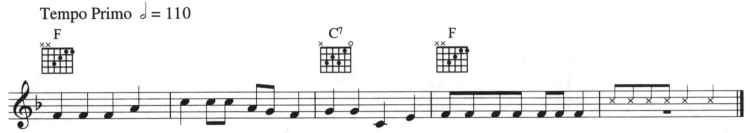

Then he died and had to be-gin a-gain, Poor old Mi-chael Fin-ne-gan be-gin a-gain

Morningtown Ride

Malvina Reynolds

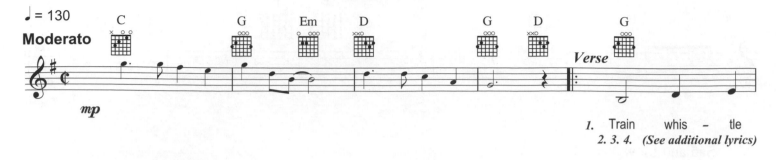

1. Train whis – tle
2. 3. 4. *(See additional lyrics)*

blow – ing, makes a sleep – y noise, un – der – neath the

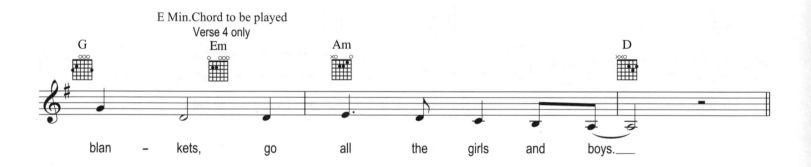

blan – kets, go all the girls and boys.___

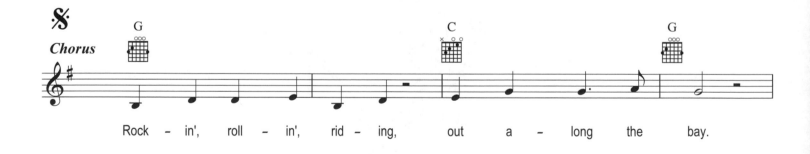

Chorus

Rock – in', roll – in', rid – ing, out a – long the bay.

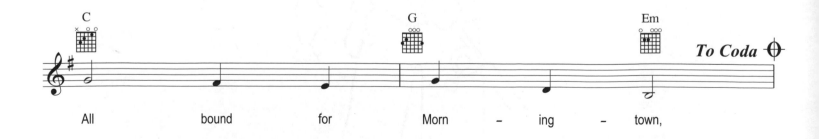

All bound for Morn – ing – town,

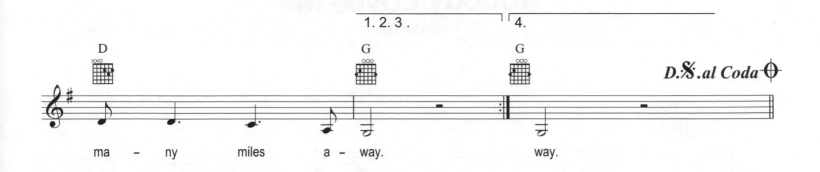

(*Additional lyrics*)

Verse 2
Driver at the Engine, Fireman rings the bell

Verse 3
Maybe it is raining, where our train will ride

Verse 4
Somewhere there is Morningtown many miles away

Nobody Loves Me

Traditional

V1) No - bod - y loves me ev - 'ry - bod - y hates me

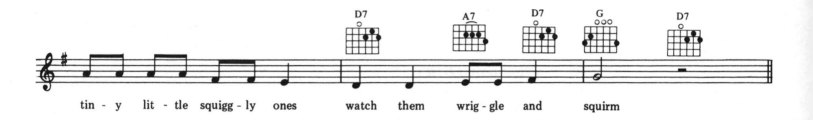

go - ing to the gard - en to eat worms Big fat jui - cy ones

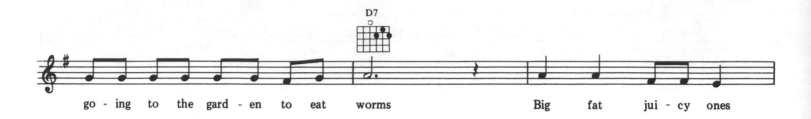

tin - y lit - tle squigg - ly ones watch them wrig - gle and squirm

V2. Bite their heads off, suck their juice out
Throw their skins away.
I don't see how birds can live on
worms three times a day.

V3. Nobody loves me, everybody hates me
going to the garden to eat worms.
Long thin slimey ones, short fat juicy ones,
Gooey, gooey, gooey, gooey worms.

V4. Long thin slimy ones slip down easily
Short fat juicy ones stick,
Short fat juicy ones stick between your teeth
and the juice goes slurp, slurp, slurp.

Oh Dear What Can The Matter Be?

Traditional

Oh Where, Oh Where Has My Little Dog Gone?

Traditional

Oh where, oh where has my lit-tle dog gone? Oh where, oh where can he be? _____ With his ears cut short and his tail cut long, oh where, oh where can he be? _____

On Your Holiday

Mathew Perry

mp

On your

Chorus

ho – li – day, on your ho – li – day, I hope you had a

To Coda ⊕

ve – ry nice time. On your ho – li – day, on your ho – li – day, I

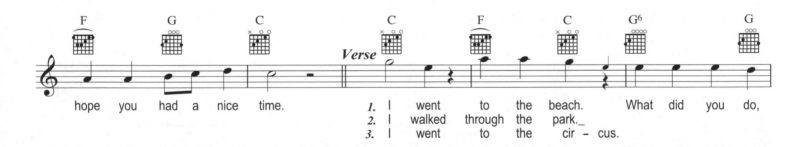

hope you had a nice time.   *Verse*

1. I went to the beach. What did you do,
2. I walked through the park.
3. I went to the cir – cus.

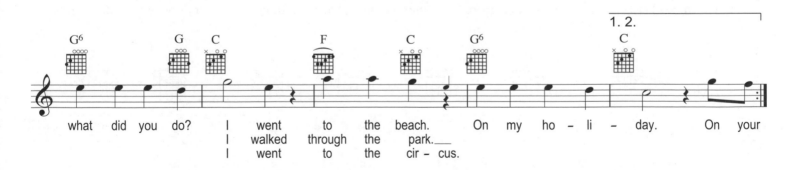

1. 2.

what did you do? I went to the beach. On my ho – li – day. On your
    I walked through the park.
    I went to the cir – cus.

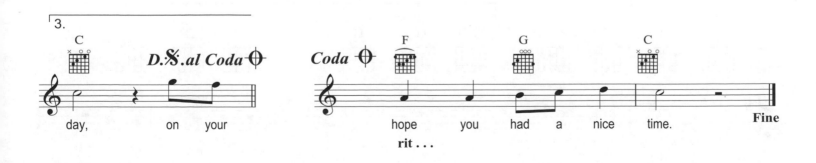

3.

D.%.al Coda ⊕   *Coda* ⊕

day, on your   hope you had a nice time.

rit . . .   **Fine**

81

Old MacDonald

Traditional

♩ = 112 Lively Hillbilly Bounce

1. Old Mac - don - ald had a farm, e - i - e - i - o. And
(Verses 2 - 5: see block lyric)

on that farm he had some cows, e - i - e - i - o. With a

moo - moo here, a moo - moo there, here a moo, there a moo, ev - 'ry - where a moo - moo.

Old Mac - don - ald had a farm, e - i - e - i - o.

1. - 4.　　　　　5.

e - i - e - i - o

Verse 2:

Old Macdonald had a farm,
E - i - e - i - o.
And on that farm he had some ducks,
E - i - e - i - o.
With a quack-quack here,
And a quack-quack there,
Here a quack, there a quack,
Everywhere a quack-quack.
Old Macdonald had a farm,
E - i - e - i - o.

Verse 3:

Old Macdonald had a farm,
E - i - e - i - o.
And on that farm he had some sheep,
E - i - e - i - o.
With a baa-baa here,
A baa-baa there,
Here a baa, there a baa,
Everywhere a baa-baa.
Old Macdonald had a farm,
E - i - e - i - o.

Verse 4:

Old Macdonald had a farm,
E - i - e - i - o.
And on that farm he had some pigs,
E - i - e - i - o.
With an oink-oink here,
An oink-oink there,
Here an oink, there an oink,
Everywhere an oink-oink.
Old Macdonald had a farm,
E - i - e - i - o.

Verse 5:

Old Macdonald had a farm,
E - i - e - i - o.
And on that farm he had some hens,
E - i - e - i - o.
With a cluck-cluck here,
A cluck-cluck there,
Here a cluck, there a cluck,
Everywhere a cluck-cluck.
Old Macdonald had a farm,
E - i - e - i - o.

Old Mother Hubbard

Traditional

Verses

3. She went to the undertaker's
    To buy him a coffin:
    But when she came back
    The poor dog was laughing.

4. She took a clean dish
    To get him some tripe:
    But when she got back
    He was smoking a pipe.

5. She went to the fishmonger's
    To buy him some fish:
    But when she came back
    He was licking the dish.

6. She went to the tavern
    For white wine and red:
    But when she got back
    The dog stood on his head.

7. She went to the fruiterer's
    To buy him some fruit:
    But when she came back
    He was playing the flute.

8. She went to the tailor's
    To buy him a coat:
    But when she came back
    He was riding a goat.

9. She went to the hatter's
    To buy him a hat
    But when she came back
    He was feeding the cat.

10. She went to the barber's
    To buy him a wig:
    But when she came back
    He was dancing a jig.

11. She went to the cobbler's
    To buy him some shoes:
    But when she came back
    He was reading the news.

12. She went to the seamstress
    To buy him some linen:
    But when she came back
    The dog was a-spinning.

13. She went to the hosier's
    To buy him some hose:
    But when she came back
    He was dressed in his clothes.

14. The Dame made a curtsey,
    The dog made a bow;
    The Dame said, your servant,
    The dog said, "Bow-wow".

Oranges And Lemons

Traditional

Pat-A-Cake, Pat-A-Cake

Traditional

Slow one-in-a-bar feel ♩. = 44

Pat - a - cake, pat - a - cake bak - er's man. Bake me a cake___ as

fast as you can. Pat it and prick it and mark it with

rit. (on repeat)

'B', and put it in the ov - en for ba - by and me.

Please Don't Call Me A Koala Bear

Don Spencer/Allan Caswell

With a swing feel. ♪ ♪ = ♪. ♪

♩ = 125

Moderato

Spoken

1. I'm a Ko - a - la, not a bear and
2. (See additional lyrics)

Verse

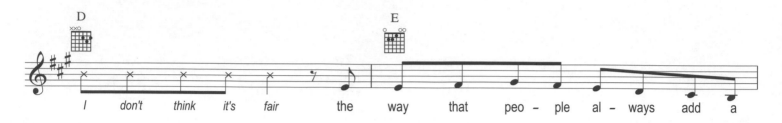

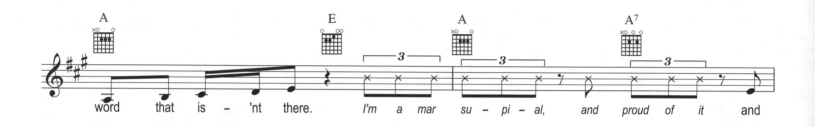

I don't think it's fair the way that peo - ple al - ways add a

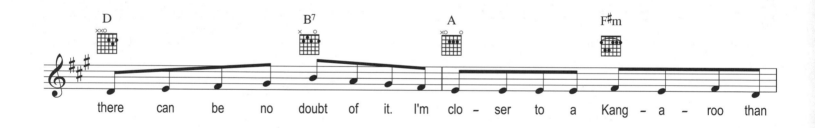

word that is - 'nt there. I'm a mar su - pi - al, and proud of it and

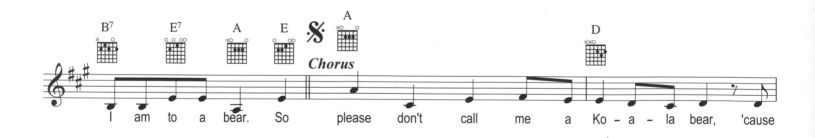

there can be no doubt of it. I'm clo - ser to a Kang - a - roo than

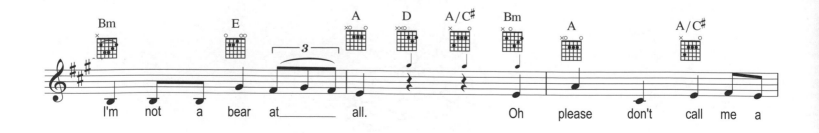

I am to a bear. So please don't call me a Ko - a - la bear, 'cause

Chorus

I'm not a bear at_____ all. Oh please don't call me a

Ko - a - la bear, it's driv - ing me up the wall. If your name was Tom and

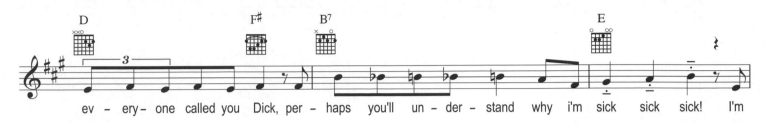

ev - ery - one called you Dick, per - haps you'll un - der - stand why i'm sick sick sick! I'm

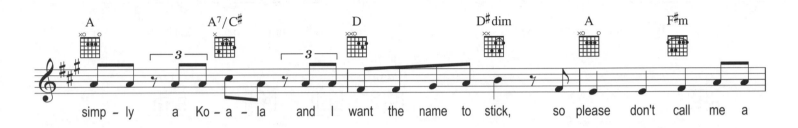

simp - ly a Ko - a - la and I want the name to stick, so please don't call me a

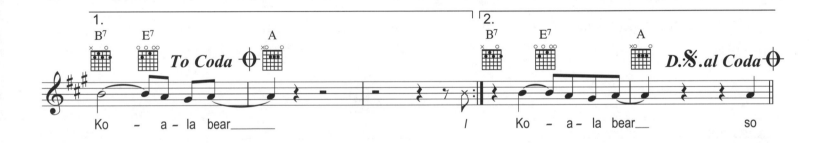

Ko - a - la bear_____ I Ko - a - la bear_____ so

89

(Additional lyrics)

Verse 2

I live here in Australia, in a eucalyptus tree,
I don't understand, fair dinkum, how anyone can think them,
Grizzly bears and polar bears are anything like me.

Polly Put The Kettle On

Traditional

Pop Goes The Weasel

Traditional

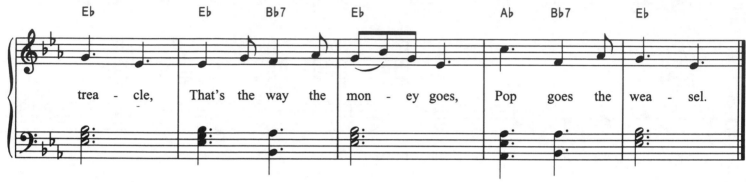

Ring-A-Ring O' Roses

Traditional

Postman Pat (Theme)

Bryan Daly

Post - man Pat, Post - man Pat,

Post - man Pat and his black and white cat. Ear - ly in the morn - ing,____

just as day is dawn - ing,____ he picks up all the post bags in his van.____

Post - man Pat, Post - man Pat, Post - man Pat and his black and white cat.

All the birds are sing - ing,____ and the day is just be - ginn - ing,____

Pat feels he's a rea - lly happ - y man.____ Ever - y - bod - y knows his

Rock-a-Bye Baby

Traditional

Rock-A-Bye Your Bear

Murray Cook/Jeff Fatt/Anthony Field/Greg Page

Romp Bomp A Stomp

Murray Cook/Jeff Fatt/Anthony Field/Greg Page

Row Row Row Your Boat

Traditional

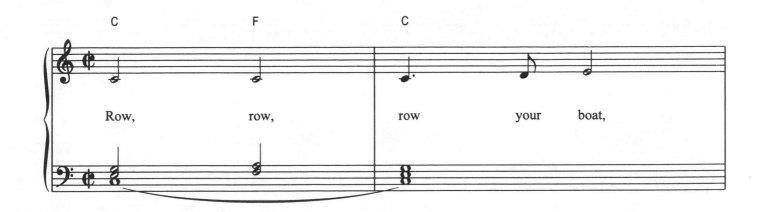

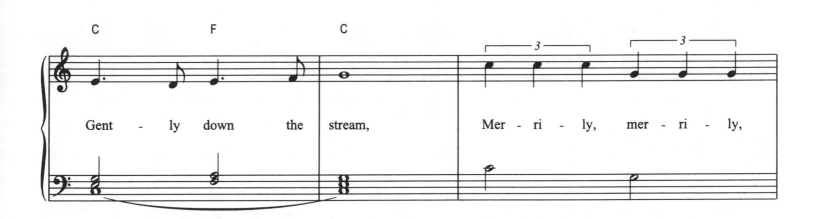

Say Hello To Daisy

P. Barton, B. O'Hara/The Flowerpot Gang

Do do do do do do do do do do do do do do do do do do do

D.%.al Coda ⊕
(Include Repeat)

instrumental

Coda ⊕

Say he – – llo!

Fine

Sesame Street (Theme)

Jon Stone/Joseph Raposo/Bruce Hart

With a swing feel.

♩ = 130

Moderato

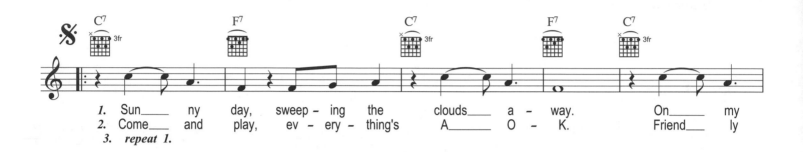

1. Sun___ ny day, sweep-ing the clouds___ a-way. On___ my
2. Come___ and play, ev-ery-thing's A___ O-K. Friend___ ly
3. *repeat 1.*

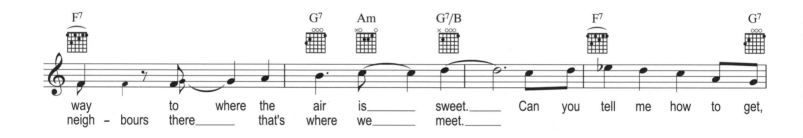

way to where the air is___ sweet.___ Can you tell me how to get,
neigh-bours there___ that's where we___ meet.___

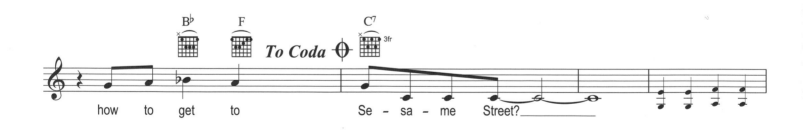

how to get to Se-sa-me Street?___

It's a mag-ic car___ pet ride,___

ev - ery door will o_____ pen wide_____ to ha - ppy peo - ple like you,_____

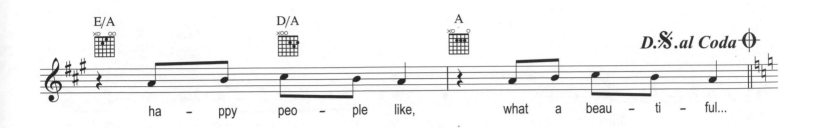

D.S. al Coda

ha - ppy peo - ple like, what a beau - ti - ful...

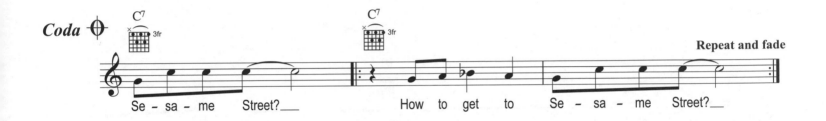

Coda

Repeat and fade

Se - sa - me Street?_____ How to get to Se - sa - me Street?_____

She'll Be Coming 'Round The Mountain

Traditional

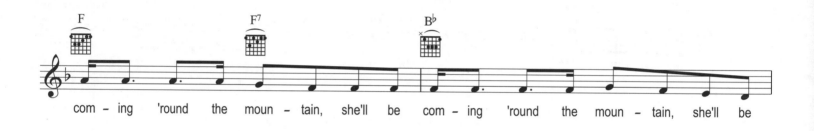

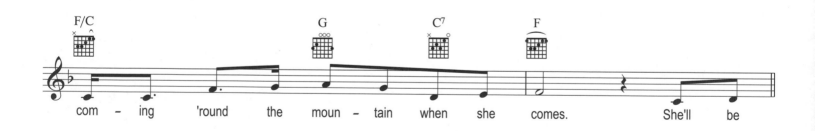

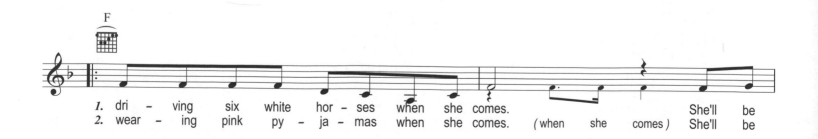

dri – ving six white hor – ses when she comes. She'll be
wear – ing pink py – ja – mas when she comes. *(when she comes)* She'll be

dri – ving six white hor – ses, she'll be dri – ving six white hor – ses, she'll be
wear – ing pink py – ja – mas, she'll be wear – ing pink py – ja – mas, she'll be

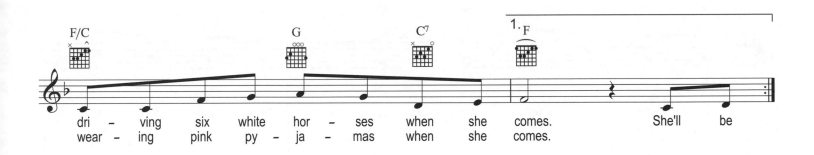

dri – ving six white hor – ses when she comes. She'll be
wear – ing pink py – ja – mas when she comes.

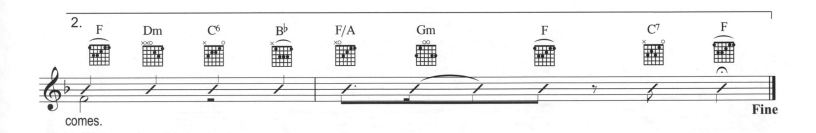

comes.

Fine

Simple Simon
Traditional

Skippy The Bush Kangaroo (Theme)

Eric Jupp

Sing A Song Of Sixpence

Traditional

Sing a song of six - pence a pock - et full of rye,

Four and twen - ty black - birds baked in a pie. When the pie was o - pened the

birds be - gan to sing, Was - n't that a dain - ty dish to

Six White Boomers

Rolf Harris/John D. Brown

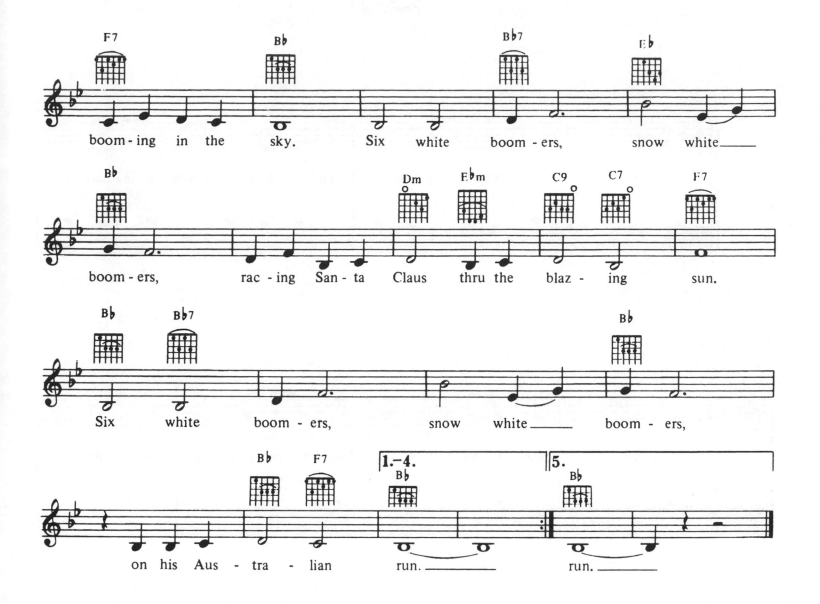

boom-ing in the sky. Six white boom-ers, snow white____ boom-ers, rac-ing San-ta Claus thru the blaz-ing sun. Six white boom-ers, snow white____ boom-ers, on his Aus-tra-lian run.____ run.____

2. Pretty soon old Santa began to feel the heat,
   Took his fur lined boots off to cool his feet,
   Into one popped Joey, feeling quite O.K.,
   While those old man kangaroos kept pulling on the sleigh.

3. Joey said to Santa, "Santa what about the toys?
   Aren't you giving some to these girls and boys?"
   "They've all got their presents son, we were here last night,
   This trip is an extra trip, Joey's special flight."

4. Soon the sleigh was flashing past right over Marble Bar.
   "Slow down there" cried Santa, "It can't be far,
   Come up on my lap here son, and have a look around."
   "There she is that's Mummy, bounding up and down."

5. Well that's the bestest Christmas treat that Joey ever had.
   Curled up in mother's pouch all snug and glad.
   The last they saw was Santa heading Northward from the sun.
   The only year the boomers worked a double run.

Skip To My Lou

Traditional

Lou,   Lou,   Skip to my Lou,   Lou,   Lou,   Skip to my Lou,

Lou,   Lou,   Skip to my Lou,   Skip to my Lou, my   dar - ling.

1. Lost my part - ner, What - 'll I   do?   Lost my part - ner, what - 'll I do?

Lost my part - ner, What - 'll I do? Skip to my Lou, my dar - ling.

Lou, Lou, Skip to my Lou. Lou, Lou, Skip to my Lou,

Lou, Lou, Skip to my Lou, Skip to my Lou my dar - ling.

2. I'll find another one, prettier than you…
3. Little red wagon, painted blue…
4. Can't get a red bird, a blue bird'll do…
5. Cows in the meadow, moo, moo, moo…
6. Flies in the meadow, shoo, shoo, shoo…

Teddy Bear, Teddy Bear

Traditional

Ted - dy Bear, Ted - dy Bear, turn a - round, ___ Ted - dy Bear, Ted - dy Bear, touch the ground.
(Verse 2: see block lyric)

Ted - dy Bear, Ted - dy bear, show your shoe, ___ Ted - dy Bear, Ted - dy Bear that will do.

Ted - dy Bear, Ted - dy Bear, say good night.

Verse 2:

Teddy Bear, Teddy Bear, climb the stairs,
Teddy Bear, Teddy Bear, say your prayers.
Teddy Bear, Teddy Bear, turn off the light,
Teddy Bear, Teddy Bear, say good night.

Ten In The Bed

Traditional

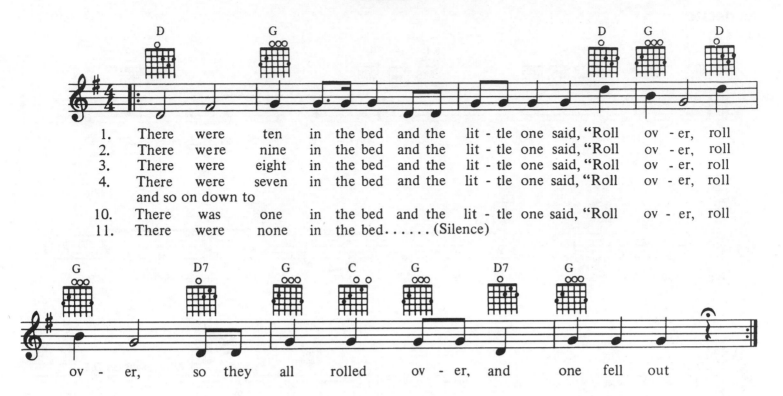

1. There were ten in the bed and the lit - tle one said, "Roll ov - er, roll
2. There were nine in the bed and the lit - tle one said, "Roll ov - er, roll
3. There were eight in the bed and the lit - tle one said, "Roll ov - er, roll
4. There were seven in the bed and the lit - tle one said, "Roll ov - er, roll
and so on down to
10. There was one in the bed and the lit - tle one said, "Roll ov - er, roll
11. There were none in the bed . . . . . . (Silence)

ov - er, so they all rolled ov - er, and one fell out

Teletubbies Say "Eh-Oh!" (Theme)

Andrew McCrorie

Moderato

♩ = 128

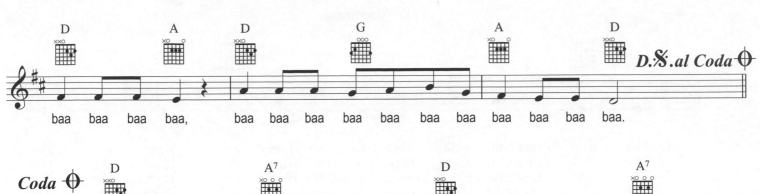

baa baa baa baa,　　baa baa baa baa baa baa baa baa baa baa baa.

Coda ✛

MA - ry　Ma - ry　quite　con - tra - ry,　how　does　your　gar - den　grow?　With

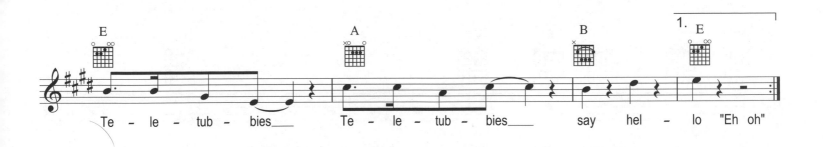

sil - ver　bells　and　cock - le　shells　and　pre - tty　maids　all　in　a　row.

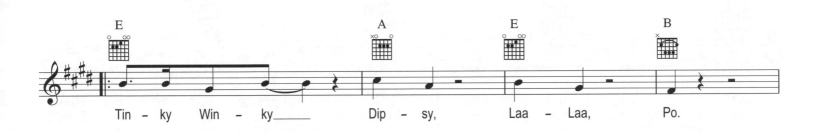

Tin - ky　Win - ky_____　　Dip - sy,　　Laa - Laa,　　Po.

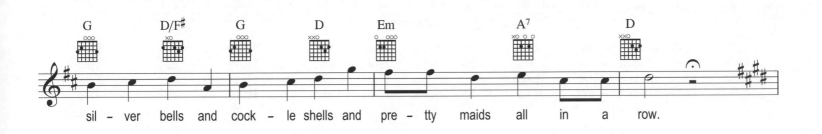

Te - le - tub - bies___　　Te - le - tub - bies___　　say　hel - lo　"Eh oh"

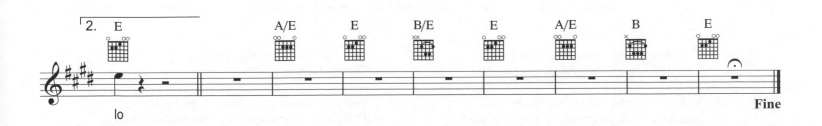

lo

Fine

The Ants Came Marching

Traditional

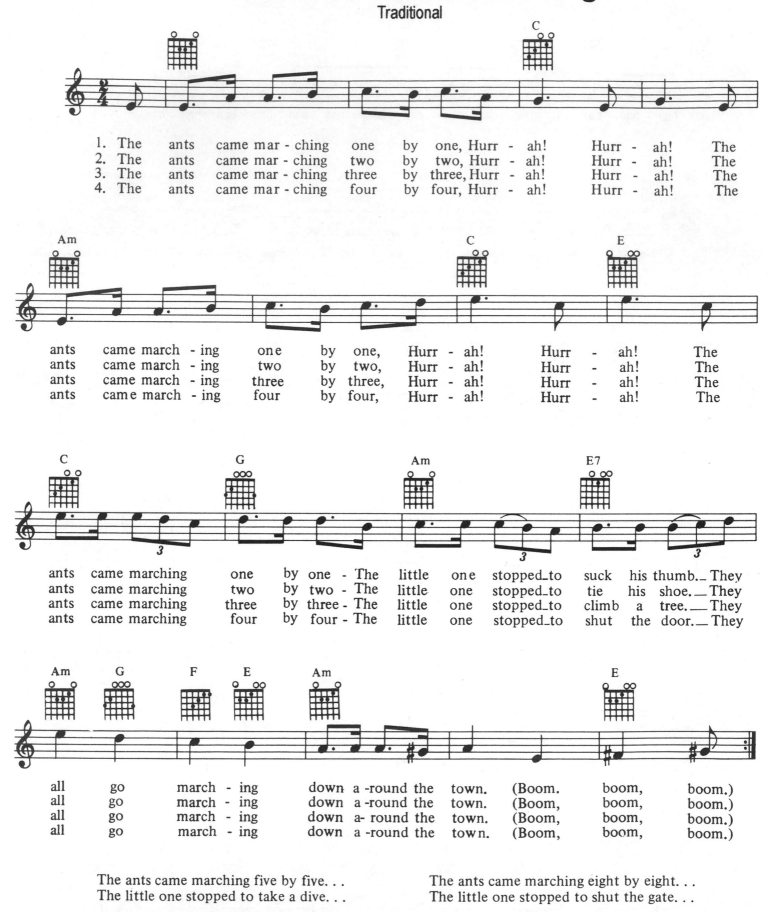

1. The ants came mar - ching one by one, Hurr - ah! Hurr - ah! The
2. The ants came mar - ching two by two, Hurr - ah! Hurr - ah! The
3. The ants came mar - ching three by three, Hurr - ah! Hurr - ah! The
4. The ants came mar - ching four by four, Hurr - ah! Hurr - ah! The

ants came march - ing one by one, Hurr - ah! Hurr - ah! The
ants came march - ing two by two, Hurr - ah! Hurr - ah! The
ants came march - ing three by three, Hurr - ah! Hurr - ah! The
ants came march - ing four by four, Hurr - ah! Hurr - ah! The

ants came marching one by one - The little one stopped to suck his thumb. They
ants came marching two by two - The little one stopped to tie his shoe. They
ants came marching three by three - The little one stopped to climb a tree. They
ants came marching four by four - The little one stopped to shut the door. They

all go march - ing down a -round the town. (Boom. boom, boom.)
all go march - ing down a -round the town. (Boom, boom, boom.)
all go march - ing down a- round the town. (Boom, boom, boom.)
all go march - ing down a -round the town. (Boom, boom, boom.)

The ants came marching five by five. . .
The little one stopped to take a dive. . .

The ants came marching six by six. . .
The little one stopped to pick up sticks. . .

The ants came marching seven by seven. . .
The little one stopped to go to heaven. . .

The ants came marching eight by eight. . .
The little one stopped to shut the gate. . .

The ants came marching nine by nine. . .
The little one stopped to scratch his spine.

The ants came marching ten by ten. . .
The little one stopped to say THE END.

The Bear Went Over The Mountain

Traditional

The Farmer In The Dell

Traditional

With a swing feel.

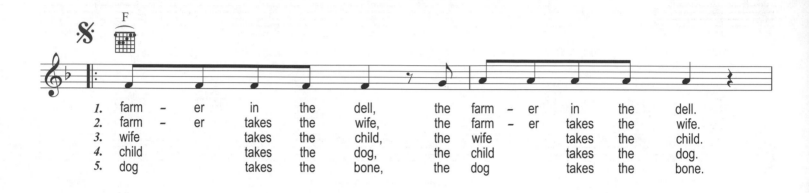

1. farm – er in the dell, the farm – er in the dell.
2. farm – er takes the wife, the farm – er takes the wife.
3. wife takes the child, the wife takes the child.
4. child takes the dog, the child takes the dog.
5. dog takes the bone, the dog takes the bone.

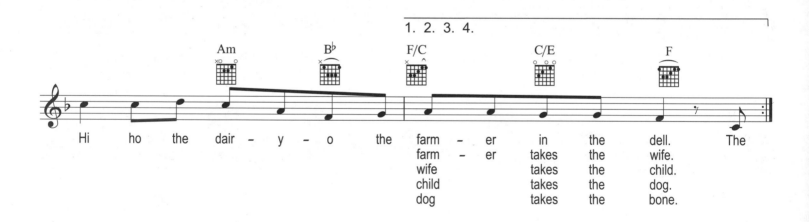

Hi ho the dair – y – o the farm – er in the dell. The
farm – er takes the wife.
wife takes the child.
child takes the dog.
dog takes the bone.

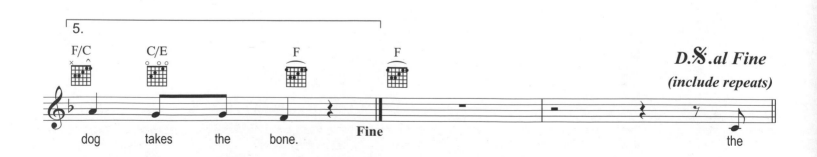

dog takes the bone. *Fine*

D.S. al Fine
(include repeats)

the

The Owl And The Pussy-cat

Poem by Edward Lear/Traditional

The Hooley Dooleys (Theme)

The Hooley Dooleys

My name's David!   Hello! My name's Antoine. And what's

your name ? <u>YOUR NAME!</u> *Oh hello!* We are the

and *how* *do* *you* *do?*

and *how* *do* *you* *do?*   **Fine**

(Additional lyrics)

Verse 2

And how are you Bruce?
I'm on top of the world and you David?
Never felt better! Antoine?
GRE...AT!
Alright!

The Teddy Bear's Picnic

John Bratton/Jimmy Kennedy

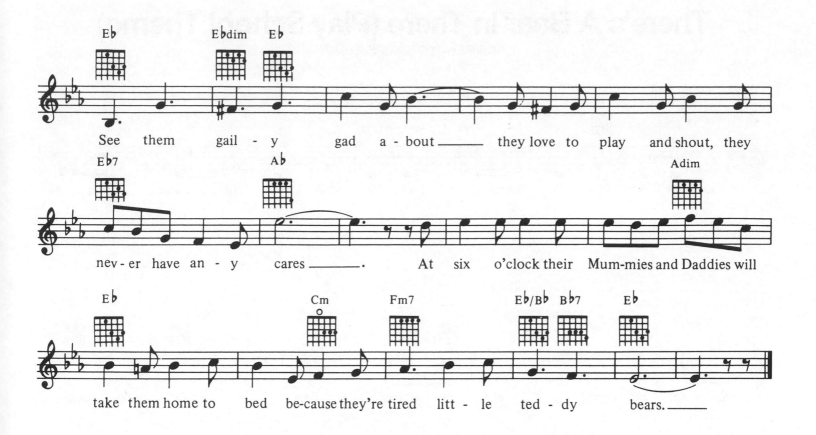

See them gail - y gad a - bout ____ they love to play and shout, they
nev - er have an - y cares ____ . At six o'clock their Mum-mies and Daddies will
take them home to bed be-cause they're tired litt - le ted - dy bears. ____

A If you go down in the woods today you're sure of a big surprise
If you go down in the woods today you'd better go in disguise
For every bear that ever there was
Will gather there for certain because
Today's the day the Teddy Bears have their picnic.

A Every Teddy Bear who's been good is sure of a treat today
There's lots of marvellous things to eat and wonderful games to play
Beneath the trees where nobody sees
They hide and seek as long as they please
'Cos that's the way the Teddy Bears have their picnic.

A If you go down in the woods today you'd better not go alone
It's lovely down in the woods today but safer to stay at home
For every bear that ever there was will gather there for certain because
Today's the day the Teddy Bears have their picnic.

B   Picnic time for Teddy Bears
The little Teddy Bears are having a lovely time today.
Watch them, catch them unawares
And see them picnic on their holiday!
See them gaily gad about
They love to play and shout, they never have any cares -
At six o'clock their Mummies and Daddies will take them home to bed
Because they're tired little Teddy Bears.

A If you go down in the woods today you'd better not go alone
It's lovely down in the woods today but safer to stay at home
For every bear that ever their was will gather there for certain because
Today's the day the Teddy Bears have their picnic.

There's A Bear In There (Play School Theme)

Richard Connolly/Rosemary Milne

With a swing feel.

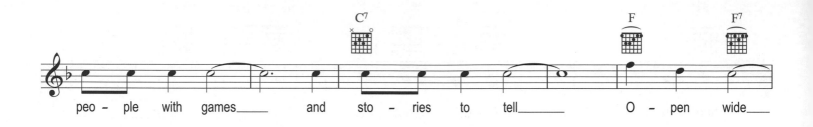

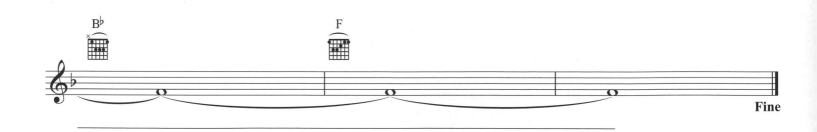

There's A Hole In The Bucket

Traditional

HENRY: But the straw is too long, dear Liza, dear Liza,
But the straw is too long, dear Liza, too long.

LIZA: Well, cut it, dear Henry, dear Henry, dear Henry,
Well, cut it, dear Henry, dear Henry, cut it.

HENRY: With what shall I cut it. . . . .

LIZA: With an axe. . . . .

HENRY: But the axe is too blunt. . . . .

LIZA: Well sharpen it. . . . .

HENRY: With what shall I sharpen it. . . . .

LIZA: With a stone. . . . .

HENRY: But the stone is too dry. . . . .

LIZA: Well wet it. . . . .

HENRY: With what shall I wet it. . . . .

LIZA: Try water. . . . .

HENRY: In what shall I fetch it. . . . .

LIZA: In a bucket. . . . .

HENRY: But there's a hole in the bucket. . . . .

Three Blind Mice

Traditional

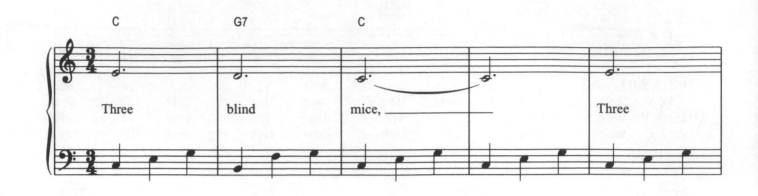

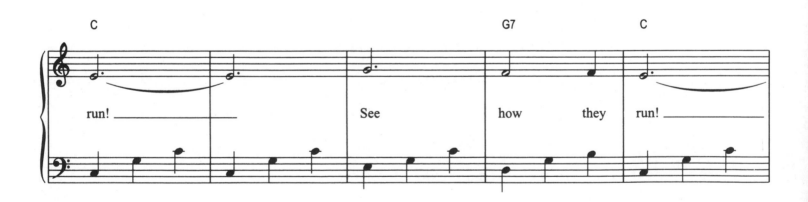

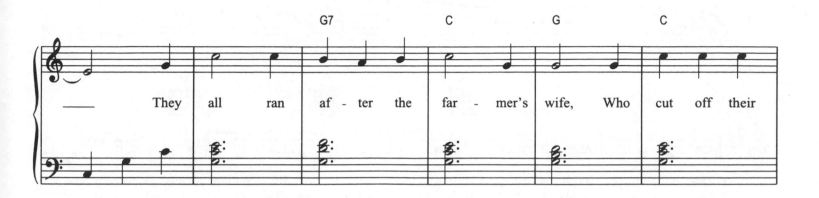

They all ran af - ter the far - mer's wife, Who cut off their

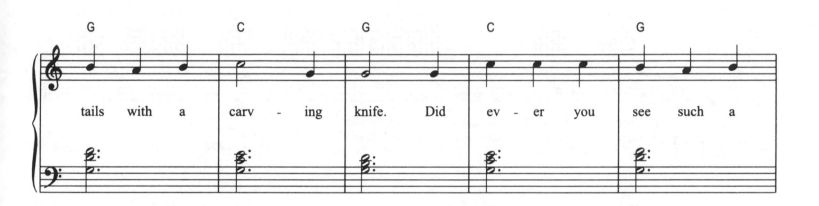

tails with a carv - ing knife. Did ev - er you see such a

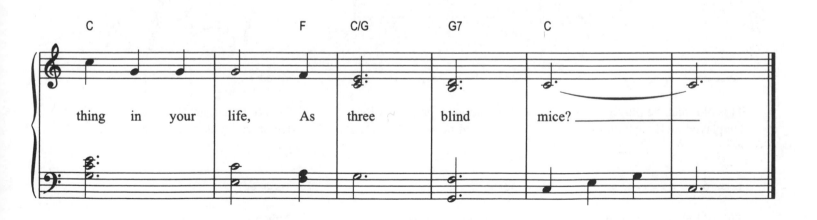

thing in your life, As three blind mice?

This Old Man

Traditional

Jolly ♩ = 104

1. This old man, he played one, He played nick-nack on my drum, With a nick-nack, pad-dy-wack,
2. This old man, he played two, He played nick-nack on my shoe, With a nick-nack, pad-dy-wack,
(Verse 3-10: see block lyric)

give a dog a bone. This old man came roll-ing home.
give a dog a bone. This old man came roll-ing home.

Verse 3:

This old man, he played three,
He played nick-nack on my knee,
etc.

Verse 4:

This old man, he played four,
He played nick-nack on my floor,
etc.

Verse 5:

This old man, he played five,
He played nick-nack on my hive,
etc.

Verse 6:

This old man, he played six,
He played nick-nack on my sticks,
etc.

Verse 7:

This old man, he played seven,
He played nick-nack up in heaven,
etc.

Verse 8:

This old man, he played eight,
He played nick-nack at my gate,
etc.

Verse 9:

This old man, he played nine,
He played nick-nack on my spine,
etc.

Verse 10:

This old man, he played ten,
He played nick-nack once again,
etc.

Tie Me Kangaroo Down Sport

Rolf Harris

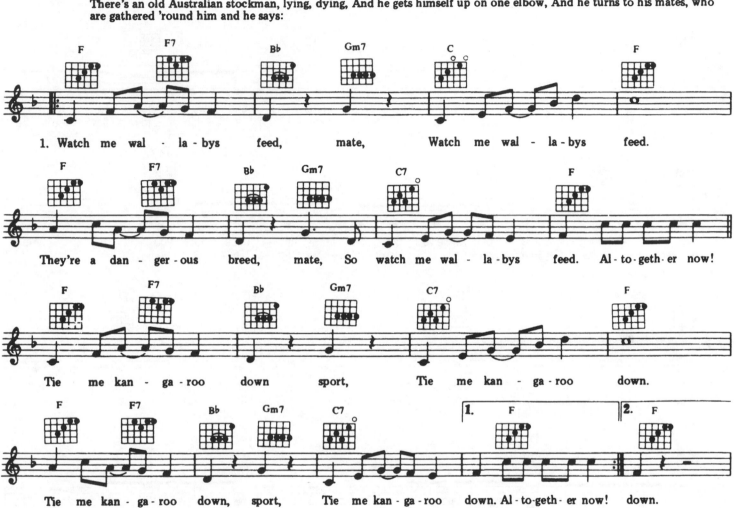

Recitation over F chord

There's an old Australian stockman, lying, dying, And he gets himself up on one elbow, And he turns to his mates, who are gathered 'round him and he says:

1. Watch me wal - la - bys feed, mate, Watch me wal - la - bys feed.

They're a dan - ger - ous breed, mate, So watch me wal - la - bys feed. Al - to - geth - er now!

Tie me kan - ga - roo down sport, Tie me kan - ga - roo down.

Tie me kan - ga - roo down, sport, Tie me kan - ga - roo down. Al - to - geth - er now! down.

2. Keep me cockatoo cool, Curl,
   Keep me cockatoo cool.
   Don't go acting the fool, Curl,
   Just keep me cockatoo cool. .
   Altogether now!

3. Take me koala back, Jack,
   Take me koala back.
   He lives some where out on the track, Mac,
   So take me koala back.
   Altogether now!

4. Let me abos go loose, Lew,
   Let me abos go loose.
   They're of no further use, Lew,
   So let me abos go loose.
   Altogether now!

5. Mind me platypus duck, Bill,
   Mind me platypus duck.
   Don't let him go running amok, Bill,
   Mind me platypus duck.
   Altogether now!

6. Play your didgeridoo, Blue,
   Play your didgeridoo.
   Keep playing 'til I shoot thro' Blue,
   Play your didgeridoo.
   Altogether now!

7. Tan me hide when I'm dead, Fred,
   Tan me hide when I'm dead.
   So we tanned his hide when he died Clyde,
   (Spoken) And that's it hanging on the shed.
   Altogether now!

Three Cheers For Paddington Bear

B. Corbett/J.de Plesses/A. Alberts

Chorus

Say hell – o to Pad – ding – ton, your new friend Pad – ding – ton,

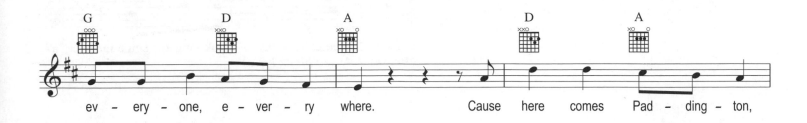

ev – ery – one, e – ver – ry where. Cause here comes Pad – ding – ton,

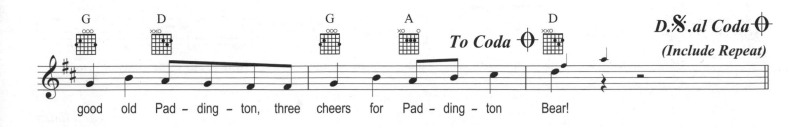

good old Pad – ding – ton, three cheers for Pad – ding – ton Bear!

To Coda

D.S. al Coda
(Include Repeat)

Coda

Chorus

Say hell – o to Pad – ding – ton, your new friend Pad – ding – ton,

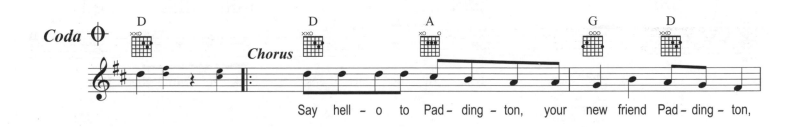

ev – ery – one e – ver – y where. Cause here comes Pad – ding – ton,

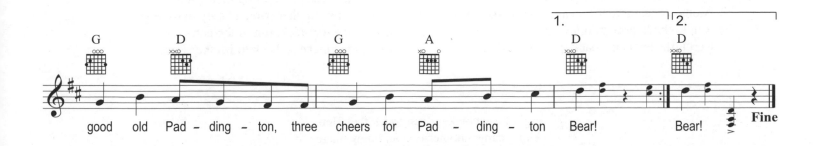

good old Pad – ding – ton, three cheers for Pad – ding – ton Bear! Bear! Fine

Two Little Chickens

Traditional

1. Two lit-tle chick-ens look-ing for some more, a-
(Verses 2-4: see block lyric)

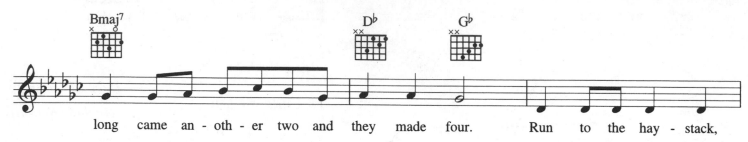

long came an-oth-er two and they made four. Run to the hay-stack,

Repeat 3 times

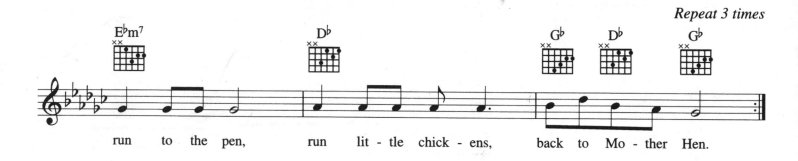

run to the pen, run lit-tle chick-ens, back to Mo-ther Hen.

Repeat and fade

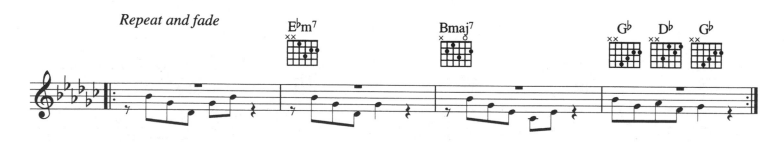

Verse 2:

Four little chickens getting in a fix,
Along came another two and they make six.
Run to the haystack, run to the pen,
Run little chickens, back to Mother Hen.

Verse 3:

Six little chickens perching on a gate,
Along came another two and they make eight.
Run to the haystack, run to the pen,
Run little chickens, back to Mother Hen.

Verse 4:

Eight little chickens run to Mother Hen,
Along came another two and they make ten.
Run to the haystack, run to the pen,
Run little chickens, back to Mother Hen.

Twinkle, Twinkle Little Star

Traditional

Wee Willie Winky

Traditional

Where Is Thumbkin?

Traditional

Where is Thumb - kin? Where is Thumb - kin?

Here I am, here I am. How are you this morn - ing?

Ve - ry well, I thank you. Run and hide, run and hide.

Verse 2:
Where is pointer? Where is pointer?
Here I am, here I am.
How are you this morning? Very well, I thank you.
Run and hide, run and hide.

Verse 3:
Where is tall man? Where is tall man?
Here I am, here I am.
How are you this morning? Very well, I thank you.
Run and hide, run and hide.

Verse 2:
Where is ring man? Where is ring man?
Here I am, here I am.
How are you this morning? Very well, I thank you.
Run and hide, run and hide.

Verse 4:
Where is pinky? Where is pinky?
Here I am, here I am.
How are you this morning? Very well, I thank you.
Run and hide, run and hide.

Verse 5:
Where's the whole family?
Where's the whole family?
Here we are, here we are.
How are you this morning? Very well, we thank you.
Run and hide, run and hide.

Wags The Dog

Murray Cook/Jeff Fatt/Anthony Field/Greg Page/John Field

Wake Up Jeff!

Murray Cook/Jeff Fatt/Anthony Field/Greg Page

Wake up Jeff, ev - ery - bo - dy's wigg - ling. Wake up Jeff, we

real - ly need you.____ Wake up Jeff, you're miss - ing all the fun now.

Wake up Jeff, be - fore the day's through!

1. What's that sound? I can
2. **Guitar Solo**
3. Do - ro - thy the Din - o - saur is

hear some - bo - dy snor - ing. What's that sound? It's not Mur - ray or Greg.____
munch - ing on some ro - ses, Wags the Dog____ is dig - ging up bones._

An - thon - y's a - wake, so let's have a - no - ther guess now
Hen - ry the Oc - to - pus is danc - ing round in cir - cles,

Oh my good - ness, it must be Jeff!
Wake up Jeff we need you for the show!

Wake up Jeff, ev – ery – bo – dy's wigg – ling. Wake up Jeff, we

real – ly need you.____ Wake up Jeff, you're miss – ing all the fun now,

Wake up Jeff, be – fore the day's through!

We Are The Saddle Club

Tim Butt/Lenore Betteridge

Welcome To The Blue House (Theme)

Bill Obrecht/Peter Lurye

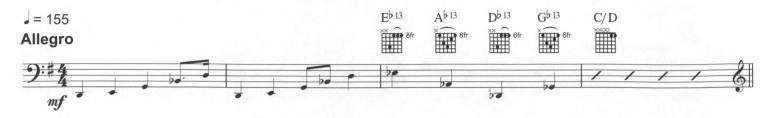

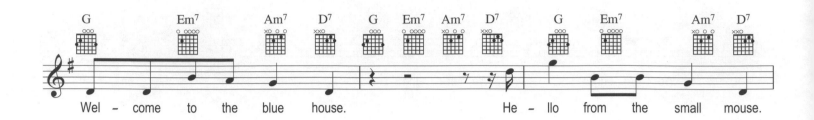

Wel - come to the blue house. He - llo from the small mouse.

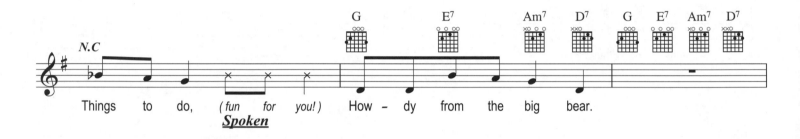

Things to do, (fun for you!) How - dy from the big bear.

Spoken

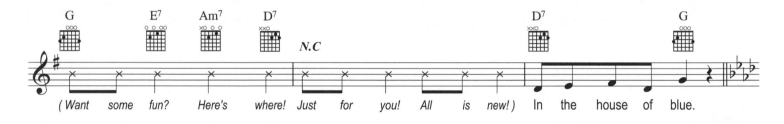

(Want some fun? Here's where! Just for you! All is new!) In the house of blue.

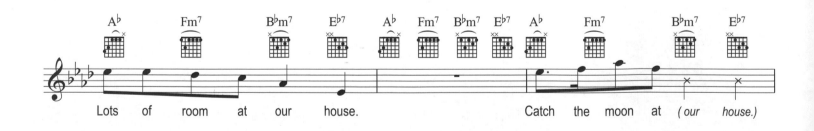

Lots of room at our house. Catch the moon at (our house.)

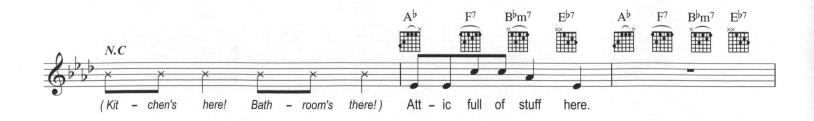

(Kit - chen's here! Bath - room's there!) Att - ic full of stuff here.

(Pi - llows full of fluff here. Whoop - de - doo! Just for you!) In the house of blue.

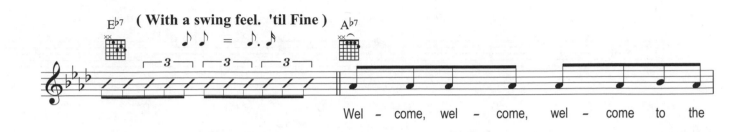

Wel - come, wel - come, wel - come to the

big blue house._ Wel - come, wel - come, wel - come to the big blue house._

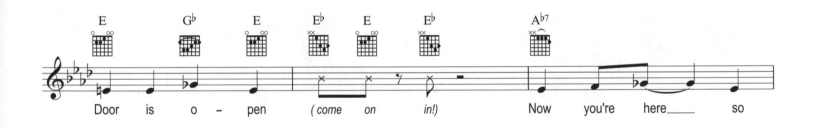

Door is o - pen (come on in!) Now you're here____ so

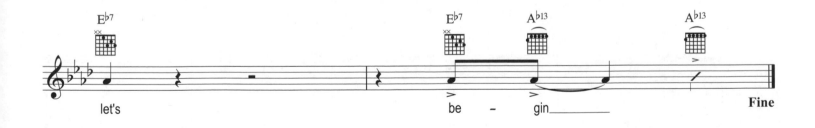

let's be - gin_____ Fine

145

Yankee Doodle

Traditional